DATE DUE

To my darling Christ⎯⎯⎯⎯⎯⎯⎯⎯⎯⎯⎯⎯⎯⎯⎯d,
Adam and Beth (and⎯⎯⎯⎯⎯⎯⎯⎯⎯⎯⎯⎯⎯⎯⎯s,
all my colleagues,⎯⎯⎯⎯⎯⎯⎯⎯⎯⎯⎯⎯⎯⎯⎯e
professionals who ha⎯⎯⎯⎯⎯⎯⎯⎯⎯⎯⎯⎯⎯⎯o
has ever offered me⎯⎯⎯⎯⎯⎯⎯⎯⎯⎯⎯⎯⎯⎯n
understanding ear to⎯⎯⎯⎯⎯⎯⎯⎯

D1419385

Foreword

In August 2011 aged 29 I was diagnosed with a Desmoplastic Small Round Cell Tumour (DSRCT). This is a rare, aggressive form of sarcoma and my disease was very advanced when I initially presented with liver and bone involvement, and an obstructive uropathy secondary to a huge pelvic mass. In my first book *The Other Side* I tried to describe my experiences as a patient through the eyes of a doctor with the hope that by reading my story other healthcare professionals would be better able to put themselves in their patient's shoes and understand what impact their behaviours, no matter how small, have on the people they look after. *The Other Side* finished with my decision to discontinue palliative chemotherapy in January 2012 which seemed like a natural ready made ending to the story.

I never originally intended to write a sequel, but many people have told me they felt *The Other Side* finished too abruptly and left them wanting to know more, so I have given in to popular demand and put pen to paper again with *The Bright Side*. It tells my story once I made that decision to stop treatment and get on with living what remains of my life. It examines my return to work and the impact illness has had on me as a doctor, my attitude to dying, the daily struggles to maintain positivity whilst living with the burden of a terminal illness and my ongoing interactions with health services as a patient including my changeable perspective on further treatment. I also hope the book challenges the societal taboo surrounding death and dying allowing for more open discussion about these important issues. I must credit Chris, my long suffering husband with the sequel's title.

In the interests of anonymity and patient confidentiality the patients I refer to in the story are fictional but have been inspired by real life people whose care I have been involved in over the past six months.

For the non-medics amongst you there is a glossary at the back of the book to hopefully explain the medical language.

The Bright Side

Get lost

It has been two weeks since I was discharged from hospital for the final time. I have delayed my clinic appointment by a week to give me chance to do a little more thinking and fully recuperate after being so ill at New Year. DtM is away and I'm seen by the female Consultant. She is not aware of the goings on during my last admission and attempts to decipher DtM's unreadable scrawl in my notes unsuccessfully. I fill her in. DtM had told me to come back to clinic when I was feeling more rational and less emotional so here I am. I still do not want to be poisoned again thank you very much. We have had a hard time explaining this decision to everyone, particularly Chris's family, but Chris himself has been brilliantly supportive and can completely understand my desire to stop with the torture. I think he was finding it increasingly distressing watching my suffering, which was consequently exacerbating his own feelings of helplessness. Most people did not really see what we were going through during the treatment as we kept it well hidden and I was only seen on rare days wearing my brave face when I felt reasonable in between cycles of chemotherapy. I am pretty good at putting the brave face on when needs be. She does not attempt to change my mind about stopping treatment and I feel our relationship is improving as I get to know her better. She seems pleased I am planning a return to work imminently.

She enquires about symptoms. I say I am "ok ish". I have been struggling with ongoing abdominal pain since New Year and it still feels like someone has kicked me in the stomach. It has taken much longer than usual for me to recover and bounce back from the last chemo cycle; perhaps this is testament to how ill I actually was. She doesn't examine me.

I have a shopping list of things I want to be done in terms of a management plan. It is nice to be back in control of things. Top of my list is the removal of my Hickman line mainly to facilitate my return to the swimming pool. I have really missed my weekly swims whilst I have been unwell. The line is now redundant and I want to get shut of it as soon as. I am keen for the procedure to be done by someone who knows what they're doing and am pleased to hear it will be performed in theatres.

I have also decided it is time for a Palliative Care referral. I finally feel ready for this. I think sorting out some Advance Care Planning would be useful and that Chris would also benefit from contact with them. I have been doing my research into who would be the best person. I know all the Consultants locally so they are all out of the question. After taking advice from some colleagues I already have someone in mind and she agrees to make the referral. We check my bloods in preparation for the line removal procedure and I ask for a 'to whom it may concern' letter about my metal stents in case they activate security alarms in airports as we have been busy booking some trips as part of the Bucket List. I have always thought it must be a nightmare to doctor me, but today I guess I have made things easier by making a sensible plan for myself. She does not add anything. When I used to clerk patients and the Consultant didn't add anything to my management plans I always viewed this as a mini victory. I decide the date I will be coming back to clinic; I have to fit this appointment into my now hectic social life.

Hurdles

Getting back to work had been an ambition since day one of becoming ill. In August DtM told me he didn't think I would work again and I have been determined to prove him wrong ever since. Being on the other side of an environment that I felt very comfortable in has been incredibly difficult for me. Sometimes in hospital I had seen things going on with the other patients and had been desperate to help out. I even used to write my own drug charts up when I was well enough. Some people would not understand my desperation to get back to work and would enjoy the freedom of a life without work given the circumstances. I however think that there are only so many times I can be a 'lady that lunches' and there is certainly only so much daytime television I can bear. I am used to a busy professional life and have put so much work into my career that it seems such a shame to throw it all away and 'retire'. I am sure that I can manage a few days a week at work, leaving me plenty of time for Bucket List activities and seeing everyone. Quite simply I love my job and always have.

In my mind it should be straightforward, I feel ready to get back to work and therefore should be allowed to. It isn't quite that simple in the Trust's eyes though and it feels like several hurdles are being lined up in front of me to clear. I know deep down inside all these procedures are in my best interests, but all I want to do is work. I make an appointment to see my GP and arrangements to visit Occupational Health (OH). The OH secretary is perhaps the nicest, most helpful lady I have ever spoken to, but I am going to have to wait ten days for the next appointment with the OH Consultant. This is frustrating. I am chomping at the bit to get back to work. The GP is pleased to see me well and out of hospital, without nephrostomies and at the Surgery as opposed to at home in pyjamas looking ill. He doesn't have a problem with my desire to return to work and can completely understand where I'm coming from. I think most other doctors could appreciate my viewpoint. He duly signs the Fit Note.

I meet up with my boss the following day to draw up a job plan and just to have a chat really. I bake lemon muffins for the secretaries. They have been missing their regular cake fixes. Everyone seems pleased to see me and I am in high spirits to be on the road to returning to work. It is very isolating being ill and I do not think I appreciated the social aspect of work before it was taken away from me. The boss is really supportive, but is keen that I don't over do things with my new role being supernumerary. I know this will be hard for me; I like to be in charge and in control especially since I became a Registrar. Just being an extra pair of hands isn't really in my makeup as a doctor.

Of course Human Resources want to get in on the act too. I find this slightly frustrating as they have never really acknowledged my illness despite me leaving several phone messages and emails initially. As I had had much more serious things to worry about at the time I just kept sending my sick notes in and hoped they were receiving them. They want to meet with me. A Consultant friend accompanies me; she has experience of getting back to work after a prolonged period of sick leave and I know she will stick up for me if they try playing silly beggars. The meeting room is hot and we all sit around the circular table. I am asked to share about my illness. I wrongly assume they realise that I am in a palliative situation and do not spell it out clearly. They talk about a phased return and it soon becomes clear that the Human Resources manager is thinking that I am going to get back to work full-time including on calls eventually. My friend steps in to correct her. I have to spell it out that I am dying and that I am never going to be well enough for night shifts. My desire is to work a few days a week and never set foot on the MAU ever again, I can do without all the stress.

As they realise the situation they acquire that look in their eyes, the sympathetic 'oh my god you're so young' look. I am asked if I really do want to come back which I find extremely patronising. Of course I do otherwise I wouldn't be wasting my precious time sat here would I? Once I get an idea in my head no-one is going to stand in my way, least of all NHS managers!

The Deanery folk also want to see me about becoming a Less Than Full Time trainee. This is all a little bit academic as in all likelihood I am not going to be surviving long enough to achieve my CCT unless there is some kind of miracle and me wanting to work is much more about my own sense of purpose and sanity rather than continuing with my training. However I guess if the Deanery are paying my wages the Trust cannot demand that I work more than I am capable of and I can be in charge of what I do without worrying about any external pressures. I meet one of the Associate Deans and my Training Programme Director. They are extremely supportive and agree with no bother that it is appropriate for me to become a LTFT trainee. Another hurdle cleared.

The Occupational Health Consultant keeps me waiting for at least an hour. I don't suppose I have anything better to do and I am well practised at sitting in waiting rooms by now. There are copies of the Trust Medical Journal on the coffee table and I am amused to find a case report written by myself some months ago prior to my illness about PNH in an older patient. He is a typical GP type. I have had very little to do with OH before other than the odd blood test or vaccination. He wants to know all about my employment history and training scheme. He then goes through my medical history with a fine tooth comb and soon fills the two pieces of paper he has allocated. Going through everything in intricate detail brings it home to me how much I have actually been through in the last six months. It is only three weeks since I decided to stop chemotherapy and I get the impression he thinks it is too soon for me to return, but I am so determined he is not going to stand in my way either! He agrees a phased return and part-time work would be appropriate which I think was apparent without asking half the questions. Last hurdle cleared. The following day I'm back on the side I belong with a stethoscope hanging round my neck again.

First Day Back

I open my first patient's case notes. My heart sinks. She has just been diagnosed with metastatic breast cancer. She has brain metastases and is confused so is completely unaware of the diagnosis. Her husband is coming in this morning for a chat about the results. I had thought by returning to the Stroke Unit that I maybe would be shielded from cancer patients a little, but clearly not. I was unsure what my emotional response to them would be. I take a deep breath, put my professional 'I am a doctor' hat on and get to work. It's amazing how easily I slip right back into doctor mode despite it being a long six months without any patient contact. After a quick assessment, I ascertain the patient has absolutely no idea of the gravity of the situation. She doesn't even know where she is. Perhaps it is kinder that way, sometimes I wish I didn't know all the details I do about my illness. Her husband is lovely, but the news comes as quite a shock to the poor man, he thought she'd had a stroke. I struggle with the conversation but I think he can see that I completely understand how he is feeling. He doesn't ask me any personal questions though. At least my empathy for the situation is true.

There is a commotion around the next bed when I return from having my difficult talk. The curtains are drawn and the house officer looks flustered grasping onto a blood gas syringe. The Consultant is trying to direct the care of the patient who is clearly not very well. I think he feels obliged to shield me from this emergency situation as it is my first day back, but I'm keen to roll my sleeves up and crack on. The Consultant looks relieved and disappears in a flash. It's just like riding a bike. I haven't looked after a peri-arrest patient for six months but I still know exactly what needs to be done. I had been worried that my skills and knowledge would have somehow disappeared. The chap has acute pulmonary oedema and the nurses are extremely responsive to my requests for oxygen, diuretics and GTN. He responds well and the initial MEWS of 6 falls to 1 in the space of an hour. I am now much more aware of the need to communicate with patients given my experiences. I try to reassure and explain to him exactly what we are doing. As I sit and write up the notes I feel useful and that my life has purpose again, such a big part of me has been missing for all these months.

The next chap on the ward round has come in with a headache, vomiting, photophobia and neck stiffness. His inflammatory markers are massively elevated. He needs a lumbar puncture. I supervise our FY2 performing the procedure. I'm very glad he succeeds as my peripheral neuropathy caused by the vincristine is still an issue and I'm not sure I would want to attempt procedures myself just yet. His CSF is so cloudy; I have never seen anything quite like it. The lab confirms a bacterial meningitis type picture. We cannot confirm the organism as he has already had some antibiotics. The contact tracing begins. My FY2 takes responsibility for this and together we write plenty of outpatient prescriptions for rifampicin. I sneakily phone the HPA for myself, my neutrophil count was only 0.9 at clinic on Monday and I could do without an episode of meningitis to contend with. "What would you recommend for an immunosuppressed doctor?" They sensibly advise prophylaxis.

What a morning, not exactly easing myself back into practice, but hey ho. I leave the ward at 1pm buzzing and invigorated. It feels wrong to be walking away after only half a day and I don't feel tired at all, but I had promised Occupational Health and Chris that I would take things easy at first and I guess I should stick to my phased return properly.

The List

There has been a great deal of talk about my Bucket List and I guess I should explain. 'The Bucket List' was a film released some years ago starring Jack Nicholson and Morgan Freeman who both played terminally ill cancer patients. The film depicts how they went about living their lives to the full and achieving things they never thought possible in their dying days. I began to compile my own Bucket List in hospital soon after I discovered the metastatic nature of my disease. I wanted an attainable list that would bring me and my family happiness and create some fond memories that were nothing to do with the illness. It would have been all too easy to be unrealistic and say that I would have liked to fly off to faraway exotic climes or jump out of a plane, but I was always very clear that my list would be filled with achievable activities.

There were some bigger things and some smaller more inconsequential things to other people on the original list. Top of the list was my desire to get married again. I loved our wedding day so much the first time round, it seemed like a lovely idea to renew our wedding vows and have a big party for all the people who have supported us so well over recent months. I also decided that I would like to travel a little. Trips to Edinburgh, London, Paris, Barcelona and less exciting places like the East Coast, the Lake District and Anglesey were added to the list. Reminiscence was also a big part of it and I wanted to recreate some of my childhood memories; a visit to the zoo, a cricket match, a steam train ride, eat fish and chips at the seaside, walk in the countryside and cook bacon on a camp stove in the moors. I decided that I have never done anything that rebellious in my life and that had to change so I would get a tattoo; nothing garish, just something small and pretty, maybe a butterfly. I wanted to buy a full price handbag in the Radley shop and to attempt to learn Italian.

I challenged myself to raise a substantial amount of money for a small local charity. Publishing my book and donating the profits seemed like a good solution to that item on the list. We chose the Yorkshire Cancer Centre (YCC) as our charity to support as the environment is so lovely at the Bexley Wing and we felt it would be nice to contribute to it in some way. Chris has got on board with the fundraising too by nominating the YCC as his work's charity of the year and by walking the West Highland Way, a very long 96 miles. The charity work keeps us both very busy, but gives us a wonderfully positive focus and a sense of achievement.

Some other things have made it onto the list quite by the chance. The biggest of these is a flight in a glider. This is something I would never have considered doing before I was ill as I am absolutely petrified of heights. However, the opportunity arose to do it and I didn't really think twice about it. There are also those things that I have always meant to do but never got round to for whatever reason. These include arranging a school reunion, going to a rehearsal of the wind band I used to play with and catching up with friends I haven't seen in years.

We achieved some of the smaller things on the list such as the Edinburgh trip whilst I was having treatment and it gave me some niceness to look forward to in between the nastiness of chemotherapy cycles. Once I decided to stop treatment the Bucket List has become a big motivator of how we spend our free time productively. I intend to keep making additions to the list as and when we think of things we would like to do.

Out

The day after my first day back at work I return to St James's to have my Hickman line removed. I sit for ages in the waiting room before the nurse calls me through for a pre-assessment. He is very chatty and it seems as though he asks me all the questions twice. No I'm not allergic to anything, no I'm not taking any anti-platelet or anticoagulant medication, yes my bloods were done recently, yes someone is going to pick me up etcetera, etcetera. He starts to explain the procedure to me. Removing Hickman lines is probably the only mini surgical procedure that I am reasonably skilled at and I have removed numerous lines in my years. I tell him this to save his time. He apologises for unintentionally patronising me, he hadn't realised my profession. I am then asked to sit in the waiting room again. Two long hours pass me by. I wonder if you added together all the hours I have spent sitting in waiting rooms for the past few months how many days it would equate to. My iPod classical music play-list does a grand job at keeping me calm.

Eventually they come and fetch me to get changed into a gown and take me through to the theatre. It's the same theatre where my line was inserted. I remember it vividly. The nurse practitioner is lovely with a competent air about her. I sign the form. She has a female junior doctor with her. It seems like a good environment to acquire some surgical skills with good supervision. I don't mind her having a go on me; it's a pretty straightforward procedure and relatively little that you can do wrong unless you are totally cack handed and cut through the line. I still struggle to describe the sensation of a scalpel cutting through my own anaesthetised skin. Soon the line is out and they sew me up nice and neatly with subcuticular sutures. I am made to stay in the recovery area for an hour. I feel fine and cannot understand all their fussing. I suppose nurses like to fuss. It is so much more comfortable wearing a bra in the absence of the line. I am no longer a bionic woman!

As a symbolic act when we return home Chris and I banish all the no longer required medical equipment from our bedroom. It is refreshing to have our dressing table as a dressing table again instead of a mini treatment room. I am not at all in denial about my illness, far from it, but the constant reminders around the house have been getting me down a bit.

Difficult

The following week I return to work on Tuesday morning. Sad person that I am I have been looking forward to putting my work clothes back on all weekend. I am extremely glad the line has gone; hospitals really aren't the cleanest places to be hanging around in with a ready made entry port for bugs. I was always surprised by the fact that my MRSA screening swabs were never positive as I was under the impression that colonisation was probably almost ubiquitous amongst healthcare professionals. I must have good hand hygiene.

The ward seems to be full of patients with brain tumours or massive debilitating strokes at the moment. I have always thought it strange how brain tumour patients seem to present in clusters, we'll have a little run of them, then won't see any for ages. We see a lady with a newly diagnosed frontal glioblastoma multiforme. She is unsurprisingly quite disinhibited socially. I had been wondering what patients would think of the doctor wearing a hat with no eyebrows or eyelashes, but most elderly people are extremely accepting so it hadn't worried me too much. She asks me "are you unwell too?" I'm not sure how to reply to this, but I guess i have to be honest and tell her I have just been having some chemotherapy for a rare sarcoma hoping that will put an end to the conversation. Unfortunately it doesn't. "So you're better now then?" I pause. Should I share the palliative nature of my disease with a patient? I guess she has asked and I don't want to lie so I simply shake my head. "You mean its terminal?" I nod and quickly change the subject to how we are going to sort out her headaches. Fortunately the patient has impaired cognition and doesn't remember our conversation the following day.

Our next patient has an obstructive uropathy secondary to renal calculi. His renal function is deteriorating and he has been nephrostomised for the same problem in the past. He is however very frail after suffering a TACS and has a significant pre-existing dementia. There is a debate about whether to proceed with a nephrostomy. The other Registrar on the ward makes a flippant comment about a nephrostomy being "a straightforward easy to perform and nothing to worry about" procedure. I have to step in. It might sometimes be an uncomplicated affair, but it might also not be. I should know. I spark a debate about what is in this gentleman's best interests rather than going ahead with something just because it is technically possible. We decide not to proceed; a decision the Urologists fully support. His renal function stabilises after a couple of days without sending him to our torture chamber.

I had been a little apprehensive about doing my first 'grim reaper' talk. Strangely I used to find this a very satisfying task and the difference you can make by properly preparing a family for the death of their loved one in a timely fashion is immense. I am however worried that I will now get over emotional about the situation. It is a lovely lady in her 90s who has had a massive intra-cerebral haemorrhage. She had been previously independent and having chatted to her family it sounded as though she was a game old lass enjoying a few whiskies like my Grandma. After showing some initial hopeful signs of improvement like so many of our patients she had gone on to develop an aspiration pneumonia and was now very flat and Cheyne-Stoking. We have started the LCP. Her family are waiting for me in the relative's room. It is easier than I had anticipated talking to them and the conversation goes as well as it can given the circumstances. They are very realistic and agree our focus of care should be on comfort and dignity. I am pleased they understand and accept the situation. I manage to retain my composure.

The lunchtime meeting is a struggle for me today. One of the Palliative Medicine SHOs is presenting about terminal

16

agitation. When I see the title, I wonder whether I should just get up and walk out. However, I'm sat in the middle of a row in the lecture theatre next to my boss and I don't want to cause a commotion. Everyone keeps commenting on how well I appear to be coping with everything, but listening to someone talk about something awful that could well happen to me especially if I develop acute kidney injury again is distressing. I'm glad to be going home after the talk so my distress can be hidden from the world.

How on earth did we cope?

Chris and I have been reflecting on my illness a great deal recently. Looking back over the past few months we keep asking ourselves how on earth we managed to do the things we did. The first social occasion I attended after initially being discharged from hospital was a big family barbecue at the in-laws. In addition to the usual Mirfield clan Chris's Aunty and Uncle from America were there as was his Aunty from down south and his Cousin from London with his wife and their new baby. I had donned leg bags and maxi dress in an attempt to hide the freakishness so as not to scare my nephews. I was unsure how much had been explained to Alex and Ryan. I'm sure Alex would have been able to understand my illness to some extent, but little Ryan was just too young and lacked the language skills to grasp the concepts involved. It was lovely to see everyone but I remember being totally exhausted mentally after only a couple of hours and retiring up to bed, not to sleep, but to remove myself from the situation. I was such a social animal before illness and yet after diagnosis I was quite withdrawn socially for a long time. Facing people was such an effort and struggle. Saying goodbye to the Americans was emotional, I couldn't get it out of my head that I may never see them again. I remember managing to fight the tears.

After my first proper cycle of chemotherapy was administered we went to Center Parcs with some close friends. We had booked this trip well before we discovered the illness and I was so determined I wanted to go even if it was just for one night away. Chris and I were both in need of a break and it would have been all too easy to mope around at home and do nothing when I wasn't in hospital. I still had my nephrostomies in situ. The parking attendants had noticed all the medical equipment in the car and were so understanding about the situation, letting us park by the lodge in case we had needed to leave in an emergency. Sarah and I had gone to the spa there and I had really enjoyed having a relaxing facial but I remember having to stop the therapist massaging my scalp as my hair had started coming out in clumps at this point. We played crazy golf and someone had to hold onto my drainage bags whilst I took my shots. I still did pretty well though. The boys had cooked what looked like a delicious barbecue, but I remember fighting to swallow every mouthful as my mouth had become incredibly sore. This was my first experience of oral mucositis which I was not prepared for with mouthwashes. I also had a very embarrassing episode where I ended up vomiting in the trees the lovely breakfast of scrambled eggs and smoked salmon Sarah had cooked for me. It took a long time for me to be able to stomach smoked salmon again. Thirty minutes after we returned home from our mini excursion I was admitted to hospital with my first episode of febrile neutropaenia.

The weekend after my antegrade ureteric stenting procedure Chris took me up to Edinburgh for a weekend away. I trained in Edinburgh and we had done the long distance relationship thing for four years between there and Yorkshire, so it will always be a special city to both of us. His Mum and Dad had given us some money and according to our new 'live for the day' philosophy we had decided to blow it on some proper luxury. Therefore we had travelled first class on the train and when we arrived Chris surprised me with a chauffeur driven Range Rover tour of the city. This was amazing as not only visiting our old favourite haunts, the driver took us to hidden parts of the city that I would have never thought to go to. I still needed to wee frequently after being re-plumbed and there was lots of toilet mapping going on. Chris has always been such a good blagger, he played the 'my wife is really ill and spent her 30th birthday in hospital' card and managed to get our suite at the Scotsman upgraded to the Penthouse. It was seriously bigger than our house, cost £900 a night and had its very own sauna and balcony overlooking the castle. I remember doing too far much physically that weekend and by the Sunday lunchtime I was really struggling with abdominal pain. We decided that the cinema would be a good way to pass the time until our train and it was the first time we had been since I was diagnosed. Before illness we used to go the cinema every two or three weeks and returning to a beloved past-time was so lovely.

The week before Christmas a 'Ponte Carnage' meal was scheduled. I should explain 'Ponte Carnage' is a group of doctors who worked together at Pontefract General Infirmary a few years ago and have kept in touch for social events. The group is very dynamic and other people have joined over the years. My friend Anshu had invited me to the meal and I remember being slightly reluctant and apprehensive about attending, but Anshu had reassured and encouraged me to come and I didn't want to miss out on dinner at Brasserie Forty Four, one of my favourite restaurants in Leeds. I had only been discharged from hospital the previous day and was taking metronidazole so couldn't drink but I was still determined to go. I had asked Anshu to make sure everyone who was coming was briefed about my situation. Unfortunately he had assumed one girl who came along would have already known, but she didn't. She is a very bubbly character. "Oh my god Kate I haven't seen you for ages, how are you? Where are you working now?" I was tongue tied, how do you explain in a noisy pub that the reason I was wearing a hat and had lost loads of weight was that I had an advanced incurable malignancy? She was just as lost for words as I was for a moment, but the awkwardness soon subsided. I had a fantastic night and didn't get home until well after midnight. There were times during my illness initially when I had thought to myself that nights like that would have never been feasible again.

Looking back it was not just the trips and social events that I do not know how we coped with. Simple things like cooking a meal with my friendly nephrostomies present were such an effort. I love to cook and bake, but much of the pleasure I got from this was taken away when I was nephrostomised. It was such an effort to only have one hand available to carry things, to bend down to put something in the oven or to reach something out of a cupboard. Even the simplest activity of daily living such as having a shower had to be a military planned operation.

Author

I never really thought I would ever finish, let alone publish *The Other Side*. When I was writing I didn't know how it was going to finish, but my decision to stop chemotherapy gave me a natural ready made ending to the story. The final scenes of the book were extremely difficult to write and I had a constant lump in my throat as I completed them. It was a big decision deciding to stop chemotherapy, but writing about it afterwards reinforced in my mind that it was the right thing for me to do. Life is so much more settled without the constant hospital interventions. I realise that chemotherapy has definitely temporarily improved my clinical situation and I am very appreciative to the Oncologists for their efforts but this time is mine now.

We read and edit the manuscript together and Chris highlights the words he does not understand so I can compile the glossary. It is the first time he has read the book and there are things in it that he didn't realise, particularly about my darkest thoughts at my lowest moments. We have a few tears. A couple of publishers have been interested, but the process was going to take ages and we would receive relatively little money for each book sold. As time is a precious commodity I do not have and the project was primarily a fundraising exercise I take someone's advice to self publish online. It is really easy and after a very fun hour of designing the cover and choosing fonts we submit the book for publishing, initially tentatively ordering one hundred copies. I'm not sure I'll manage to sell all those, but I'll give it a go.

The following week I can barely contain my excitement to get home from work and see the results. Two brown cardboard boxes are waiting for me. We open them and there it is; my book in print. Wow. A published author with an ISBN and everything! I can see in Chris's eyes he is very proud of me. I sign a few copies for family and friends. We split the remainder of the books between us to sell at our respective workplaces. It becomes clear by the end of the week we need to put another much bigger order in. My clever brother designs me a website and I post information about the book on the charity forum on Doctors.net not really thinking anyone will look at it. By the end of the day though I am the Top Quality Post and the orders are piling in. Someone tells the Medical Registrar on Facebook about me and they plug the book too. I am an avid fan of the MR and it is really weird to be a topic of discussion on their page. I guess this is my first taste of celebrity in a strange kind of way. I feel as though I am drowning in a sea of jiffy bags, but we soon get an efficient system going and we are keeping our local Post Office in business. It only takes a few weeks before I reach my seemingly ambitious initial target of 1000 books.

Who stole my self confidence?

The Geriatric Medicine regional training day is being held at my hospital this month. I am in two minds about whether to attend or not. I am not sure my illness is common knowledge yet, but I do want to sell some books and it would be nice to see some folk I've not seen in ages. I give myself a pep talk to stop being silly and face up to it. It takes a great deal of emotional energy for me to maintain the strong happy public face, especially when people who don't know about the cancer find out for the first time.

After popping onto my ward to check everything is ok first thing I wander over to the Medical Education Centre. Luckily a couple of girls who I know and have been visiting fairly frequently are already there. It is nice to see some friendly faces. They are pleased to see me back at work and I fill them in on my decision to sack the Oncologists. More people arrive. I get some funny looks; maybe they are wondering why I am wearing a hat. The talks are really interesting and it is lovely to be being educated again. My mind had been festering whilst I have been ill with only writing the book keeping it active really. Once the last presentation of the morning is over I pluck up the courage to stand up and give a short spiel about my book and the fundraising efforts. I can see the faces change as I speak, the 'oh my god' faces appear. They are all really interested though and almost everyone buys a copy. I have a hard time trying to eat my lunch as they all seem to want my autograph. I guess this is probably my first book signing event! £240 in the coffers, easy as that. I would never have thought twice about standing up in this kind of environment before, I used to be the trainee's representative and do it all the time. I find it really tough today though, the cancer seems to have stolen my self confidence in a big way. This is one of those hidden consequences of illness that we as healthcare professionals probably underestimate and do not consider enough.

The following week I attend the GIM training day in Hull. Anshu gives me a lift and I'm glad not to be alone as my confidence is still sadly lacking. I receive several hugs as we arrive and soon start to feel reasonably comfortable in myself though. Some people I know seem to avoid speaking to me; perhaps they don't know what to say. When I first became ill I was disconcerted by the fact that I knew people were talking about me and the NHS rumour mill was working overtime. I think it was probably a control thing in that I was unable to control information about me spreading around. I knew that no-one meant any harm by the gossip but it still distressed me and I only told a few colleagues who I really trusted about my illness. Given the fact that I have now committed my experiences to paper I can no longer expect any privacy.

The first talk is all about the gastrointestinal complications of chemotherapy and the speaker asks the audience about the pathophysiology of chemotherapy related vomiting. I know all about that! I stay quiet though; my confidence is not good enough to speak up in this environment yet. He does not mention levomepromazine, the only truly effective anti-emetic in my experience. Some of the Geriatrics clan chat about what they thought of *The Other Side* at the coffee break. This is first direct feedback from doctors I have received and everyone seems really positive that the story has changed their practice for the better in so many different ways. I am truly humbled by this.

Pragmatic stoicism

I have become very pragmatic and matter of fact about my own impending mortality over recent months. I have always accepted the fact that my life is going to be cut short since I discovered my illness and I have never really felt angry about the whole situation. People around me seem to struggle with my attitude at first. One of our nurses says "you can't say that," in response to me jokily saying that I wouldn't be around in a couple of months to follow-up on something in clinic. They soon learn to accept my outlook though. They have to. I am cheerful and outwardly happy. Life is what it is, I cannot change what has happened to me or what will happen in the future and there is absolutely no point getting gloomy about it all. I have been given some precious well time and I am so determined to make the most of it but I do not want people to pussy foot around me ignoring the elephant in the room. I am therefore very open about my dying and expect those around me to be too. I regularly talk about 'popping my clogs' even to people I am not that well acquainted with and my black humour on the subject often shines through. "I'm genuinely happy at the moment and want everyone at work to have a laugh with me like the old days." One of our Stroke Assessment Nurses replies "let me get used to the idea, from tomorrow I promise to laugh with you all the way." She keeps her promise.

One of the ward nurses tells me under the influence of a little alcohol whilst we are out on the ward 'ale trail' afternoon that she cannot understand my change in personality since I have become ill. She says she always liked and respected me before but that I have changed and now brighten up the Unit with my smile and giggling. She cannot comprehend how I can appear so happy when I am so ill. I'm not sure how to respond to this. I guess I just don't let things get to me anymore and enjoy life for what it is.

In a way I feel lucky to know roughly when my own death will occur so I can prepare properly for it. I have been writing letters to everyone I care about for when I do die telling them what they mean to me, making a memory box for Chris and ensuring my affairs are in order. I have always been a practical person so my will is signed and sorted, and my funeral plan is finished. I have even sorted my old clothes out a bit so there is less for Chris to do. So many people die suddenly and are never given the opportunity to organise things. I feel more peaceful that these tasks are complete and I can now park them at the back of my mind and crack on with living my life.

People keep telling me how brave and inspirational they think I am. Complete strangers regularly write to me expressing these views. I am very humbled by this but I really do not agree with them. It is not about bravery in my eyes, I really have not had much choice about what I have had to deal with and I do not view my own behaviour as particularly courageous. I am just Kate. I just plough on with each day as it comes and try my very hardest to keep smiling. Someone described it as pragmatic stoicism, which is a phrase I much prefer.

Fight

I have always been an early bird at work. Having an hour to myself to organise my day and work out what has been happening on the ward is essential to everything running smoothly and me maintaining control. I have proper bad OCD at work. I soon get back into the habit of turning up before 8am again. Today almost as soon as I have taken my coat off the nurses tell me they are concerned about a patient admitted the previous day with a cerebellar haemorrhage. She had early hydrocephalus on her initial scan but had a GCS of 7 when she was admitted so the neurosurgeons had not been interested and she had basically been admitted to the Stroke Unit for some TLC whilst awaiting her demise. However, her conscious level had rapidly improved during the day; she had been talking to her family and moving all her limbs purposefully.

This morning however she has deteriorated again and her GCS is now hovering between 6 and 8. She is the same age as my Mum and was independent prior to all this. I crack on with organising a repeat urgent CT head. It confirms my clinical suspicions that her hydrocephalus is worsening and I phone the on call Neurosurgical Registrar at Leeds. He is really difficult with me as some Surgeons often are with Medics. His argument is that because the patient is DNACPR that she shouldn't be for any neurosurgical intervention, but then reprimands me for not referring to anaesthetics for intubation and ventilation. I assert myself that I am not going to ask an anaesthetist to intubate my patient if the neurosurgeons have no intention of intervening as we would then be in a palliative situation and an ICU admission would be wholly inappropriate. I cannot understand his logic and start to question my own clinical reasoning. I do feel however that a drainage procedure would be in this patient's best interests and try to articulate this to the Neurosurgeon. He cries off making the decision to go and discuss the case with his Consultant. I am reassured that my boss agrees with me. Her family are on edge and overhear my phone conversation. They can see I have been fighting hard for their Mum and I receive numerous hugs of appreciation. The Neurosurgeon phones back a few minutes later and agrees to transfer the patient for intervention. I think my own illness has definitely made me more aware of becoming my patient's advocate as well as their doctor and I think I perhaps fight harder for my patients now than in the past. I am extremely lucky to be able to advocate for myself effectively the vast majority of the time, but not all patients are this fortunate particularly in my specialty. I tried really hard to advocate for this patient today and achieve the desired outcome; there is no job satisfaction in the world like Medicine.

Struggling

I don't know how to help Chris. I have tried every strategy I have in my communication skills armoury and they have all failed. The trouble is that I have completely come to terms with the fact that in a few months I will be dying. Chris has still not accepted this fact and remains in the 'it's not fair' stage. He struggles so much with my matter of fact attitude and gets upset at the smallest of comments. I am perhaps not as sympathetic as I should be and we seem to be constantly at loggerheads recently. "Pull yourself together darling".

When he is upset he always talks about what life will be like without me and how he will not be able to cope. This is very difficult to listen to and is a source of great annoyance for me. I am the one who is dying and facing potentially a painful, protracted and horrible death, but all he seems to be able to think about is himself. Perhaps I am the one who is being selfish or perhaps it is both of us. I am such a cow.

I normally go up to bed an hour or so before Chris; he always tucks me in and gives me a good night kiss but then goes back downstairs. I have been listening to him crying to himself virtually every night during this hour since I came home from hospital. The doctor in me really wants to sort him out. The wife in me is distressed by his distress and he is probably my biggest concern at the moment. I can easily see how he may very well develop a grossly abnormal grief reaction when I do die if we do not attempt to get him to come to terms with everything sooner rather than later.

Chris does not share my black humour on the topic of dying. I flippantly make a comment that being a petrol head he would be able to buy a Porsche with my life insurance money. Chris responds "what if I don't?" I reply "I'll haunt you!" He does not find this amusing, but I guess in reality the memory of me is probably going to haunt him for a protracted period of time after my death. He has always worshipped the ground I walk on.

I have arranged a consultation with Palliative Care for both of us. Chris has not accompanied me to an appointment for a long time. I nag him into this one though; I think for context it is important we are seen together. We meet the Consultant and one of the Macmillan nurses. The room is really hot and I have far too many clothes on. It feels more like a marriage counselling session than a Palliative Care consultation. We talk about mine and Chris's fears. I have deliberately worn mascara to reduce the risk of me crying now my eyelashes are growing back. They work out some of the reasons Chris is struggling emotionally and I think talking about these openly does help him. He is so used to planning in his career that he cannot get his head around my 'live for the day' philosophy. However, when he does start to think about the future, this causes him the greatest distress. I can't help feeling like the whole meeting is akin to Alcoholics Anonymous with Chris finally admitting to some of his fears and anxieties.

We spend relatively little time considering my symptom control. I remain determined to manage this myself and am so anti opiate medication I do not think anyone is going to change my mind about this at the moment. There will come a time when I will obviously need opiates regularly again but I am nowhere near that yet. The Consultant does make a useful suggestion about radiotherapy to try and help with my bone pain though. She is so sensible and I find myself admiring her communication skills as we chat. I will be pinching some of her strategies and phrases. Radiotherapy will be top of the agenda next time I see the Oncologists.

Of all the Oncologists...

It's a busy day. The Unit is a little chaotic as the games of bed shuffling go on. One of the Stroke Assessment Nurses tells me about a patient in the Emergency Department she has seen. Her scan has shown a big intra-cerebral haemorrhage but to complicate matters she is on warfarin for a metallic mitral valve replacement. Her INR is 5.6. It's the first time I've been up to the ED since I came back to work. I know a few people there are aware of my illness. We go together, moral support for me more than anything I think. I sort out the anticoagulation reversal first. The ED is manic and perhaps unsurprisingly this has yet to be organised. I know her nurse well and the vitamin K is injected soon after I scribble the prescription. I give the Haematology ward a ring as it is a Thursday morning and I know I'll track a Consultant down there. I have not lost the ability to articulate quickly what I need; I had been a bit worried that this skill might have deserted me. The Octaplex is ordered.

The patient is very dysarthric making it difficult to get a clear history and the ED clerking is shall we say somewhat rudimentary. I ask the patient's partner about other health conditions and am told she has melanoma for which she has recently started chemotherapy. I ask to see her Bexley Wing bumf. He produces the 'how to have cancer' folder. It's just the same as mine. The treatment card says she is having dacarbazine. Her Oncologist is the female sarcoma Consultant. They look after melanoma and the weird stuff as well as sarcoma. I mutter under my breath as I leave the cubicle, "of all the bloody Oncologists in the Bexley Wing."

I pluck up the courage to ring St James's to get the letters faxed over. We really need to know what her prognosis is like and they need to know she has been admitted with a condition that is likely to cause a rapid and persistent decline in her Performance Status. When asked who to make the fax for the attention of and I say my name, I am asked "is that our Kate Granger?" I'm so embarrassed for some reason. People treat me as Dr Kate at work and I hope I am seen as a slightly bossy competent but compassionate woman with an ability to sort stuff out. I cannot stand the thought of being perceived as the poor girl who is dying of cancer. When my world of being a patient overlaps with my professional life I find it extremely uncomfortable.

After spending an hour mixing and injecting Octaplex with my FY2's assistance I decide it is time for the 'serious chat' with the patient's partner and to discuss resuscitation status especially given the advanced metastatic malignancy and severe disabling intra-cerebral haemorrhage. We go into our relative's room. I soon ascertain he has expectations that the chemotherapy is going to cure her cancer. I'm sure the Oncologists must have explained the palliative intent of the treatment and perhaps they didn't want to hear the information they were being told. However in my experience some Oncologists do have a tendency to use far too many euphemisms. I have been on the receiving end of this sort of communication and can completely see how confusing it could be. I try to correct his understanding of the situation.

Life of luxury

Chris is in his element planning the Bucket List. He loves organising things and it is giving him a fantastically positive focus. This weekend we are going to spend a fair bit of money, although I am trying not to think about how much everything is costing and am just concentrating on enjoying myself. The train is already at the platform when we arrive at the station and we take our seats in the first class carriage. They wine and dine us on the way down to London and I must have had close to half a bottle of Pinot Grigio as I feel quite tipsy walking along the concourse at King's Cross. The taxi takes us right up to the front of the Savoy and a doorman helps me out and sees to our luggage. They are expecting us and after the whistle-stop tour of where everything is we are checked in. Of course Chris has blagged an upgrade, pretending it is my birthday. The room is gorgeous, so sumptuous and decadent. No time to rest though as we have afternoon tea booked in the foyer. The surroundings are amazing, chandeliers, grand piano, crisp white table clothes and waiters wearing tail coats. Chris and I both feel a little bit common, but take our seats and try to behave appropriately and not drop anything. They have blackcurrant and hibiscus tea, my favourite, I'm definitely having that. The service is immaculate. The minute the waiters see you reaching for something they come and take over. There is so much food there is no way we will need any dinner. The cakes are a work of art and it seems a shame to eat them although they taste absolutely delicious. Towards the end of this wonderful experience the waiter brings me a plate with 'Happy Birthday' written on with chocolate and a small cake whilst the pianist plays happy birthday. Everyone claps. I blush. It's not even my birthday!

The following morning Chris tells me we are going on a tour of the hotel to look at stuff like the staff quarters and the Ball Room. We have to be outside the hotel for 10am. There is a group of people waiting outside so I assume they must be going on the tour too. Soon however a beautiful silver Rolls Royce draws up. I point it out to Chris knowing his obsession with all things car related. He asks me to come and have a look to which I reply "no I'm ok thanks darling". He insists. He's done it to me again hasn't he? Booking fancy cars to chauffeur us around. If I had known I was going in a Rolls Royce I would have worn something more suitable than jeans and trainers. I am slightly annoyed with him, but he is so excited that I guess I just need to get over my embarrassment and join in his enjoyment. The driver takes us to Windsor and around the all the Capital's sights. Tourists keep taking photos of us and the car; I think they must think we are celebrities of some sort. After a fun four hours the driver drops us off at Fortnum and Mason's, one of my favourite stores in London.

I am perhaps most looking forward to the next event which is dinner at Claridges. Having dinner at a Michelin starred restaurant was very high up on the original Bucket List so why not make it a double starred restaurant? I wish I had enough hair not to have to wear a hat, but unfortunately I don't. Never mind. At least I can wear a pretty dress. I have been wearing lots of dresses since I got rid of my nephrostomies just because I can. They seat us at the back of the restaurant in a secluded little corner. It is so intimate it literally feels like it is just Chris and I having dinner and no-one else is here. The wine list comes on an iPad; there must be thousands of bottles to choose from. We plump for a Californian Viognier in salute to our trip to the Vineyards a couple of years ago and hand the iPad back to the sommelier. They decant the wine. Wow, this is really posh, well too posh for the likes of us! I choose scallops with caviar, veal fillet with sweetbreads, vanilla and salsify and a chocolate fondant with salted caramel ice cream. We sneakily take photos of the food as it arrives. Absolutely delicious does not even come close to describing how good it tastes. We have banned talk of illness over dinner and I feel like I used to going on dates with Chris near the beginning of our relationship.

At the end of the meal the Maitre d' approaches me "Dr Granger I believe you are a big fan of cooking, would you like to see the pass?" "Yes please!" I respond excitedly. I didn't think the evening could have got any better but clearly it can. We then walk down the pass. The kitchen is immaculately clean and despite all the shouting the teams are all working so quickly yet so precisely. The head chef asks if we enjoyed dinner. I manage to nod but am a little bit star struck and overwhelmed by the experience. What a weekend. Chris has always treated me like a princess but he really pulled out all the stops this time with his escapades and I feel very happy to tick a few things off my list successfully with every experience completely exceeding my expectations. It is back to reality now though.

Getting my own way

It is six weeks since I was last at clinic. I have been living my life on fast forward recently and have lots to say about what I have been up to. I feel reasonably well and am determined to make the absolute most of this precious time with the Bucket List being well and truly under way. I am constantly busy and everyone has been commenting that they don't know how I am managing to fit everything in. I don't really know myself especially as my sleep is quite disturbed by bone pain, but I just keep going. I have no other choice. I see the female Consultant. I suggest giving radiotherapy a try as per the Palliative Medicine Consultant's suggestion and she agrees to arrange a referral to Clinical Oncology for this. My lower abdomen is tender on examination, but I am glad she cannot feel a mass yet. We have a conversation about how work is going and I tell her about her patient I am looking after with the intra-cerebral haemorrhage. I refrain from discussing the communication issues, it would not be appropriate.

I give DtM his copy of the book as I leave clinic. I have written in the front "I hope you are not offended by my portrayal of 'DtM'. Thanks for looking after me, Kate x". He seems a little puzzled by his nickname but I refuse to explain, he's a bright chap and I'm sure he'll work it out for himself soon enough. I am very apprehensive about what people who have looked after me will think of my writing, but I guess I cannot keep the book a secret from them if I want it to have any impact.

My copy of the clinic letter arrives a few days later. The Consultant states that I am Performance Status one, not zero. I swim fifty lengths once or twice a week, regularly go for five mile walks and run round like a headless chicken at work three days a week. I am probably more physically active now than I was before illness. I wonder what I have to do in

37

order to be Performance Status zero. Maybe run a marathon? I might just do that, perhaps more realistically a 10km though!

Back to GP land

I made an appointment to see the GP about a week ago primarily to stock up on analgesia prior to my radiotherapy. The waiting room is full of badly behaved snotty nosed children. I continue to hate waiting rooms. I sit and read the Mid Yorkshire End of Life Strategy (EoLS). I have joined the EoLS group and my first meeting is tomorrow. Some people might suggest this is a very challenging thing for someone who is dying to tackle. I however think I now have a unique perspective on Palliative Medicine and that I can hopefully improve care in the acute hospital in my own little way if I stick around long enough to undertake some projects.

Although I have my original agenda to get an Oxynorm prescription I've also not been feeling quite myself for a week or so. I only managed twenty five lengths at swimming on Monday when I had been able to complete fifty easily of late. I felt really quite short of breath and dizzy when I dragged myself out of the pool. I am being an annoying patient and just don't feel right in a really non-specific way, but I suppose I am riddled with cancer. My thoughts are that the symptoms are most likely related to disease progression. The GP counteracts my pessimism and sensibly wants to look for any reversible causes. We agree to send an MSU and some bloods, which I'm sure will all be normal. I am lucky to be able to get these sorted at work and follow up on the results myself. It's so much less hassle. As predicted the tests are all ok. I pick up a few days later so maybe it was just a minor blip. I must stop analysing every symptom so closely. It's really difficult though as before I was diagnosed I was relatively asymptomatic given the advanced nature of my disease so maybe I should be taking note of every little twinge. With a retrospectoscope perhaps I had been quite tired but I guess that is case for every Medical Registrar slogging their guts out day in day out in the unforgiving world of the NHS.

Zapping

I am very nervous about the radiotherapy. I'm not entirely sure why, it should be a walk in the park compared with the hardcore chemotherapy. Maybe it's because I have been away from hospital for a number of weeks and some semblance of normality has been restored to life, coming back for interventions is just another reminder that all is not well. I check in at the radiotherapy desk and am pleased to see one of my Consultant friends has come down to wait with me before my clinic appointment and have a good old natter. She has been amazingly supportive throughout this journey.

I think Oncologists must specialise in running their clinics as late as possible. It seems to apply to the Clinical Oncologists just as much as the Medical Oncologists if today's performance is anything to go by. I get really stressed when my own clinics run late and I have a waiting room full of people to see. An hour and a quarter after my scheduled appointment time the Consultant finally calls my name. Never mind, it's my day off and I suppose I have had chance to catch up on my journal reading in peace and quiet.

This Consultant is very down to earth and normal. He basically just needs to consent me for the zapping. I have done my research and I think I have a reasonable idea about what I am letting myself in for. He tells me most patients tolerate radiotherapy much better than chemotherapy. I point at my notes folder which is now bursting at the seams and say reading all that tells the story of my inability to tolerate chemotherapy. Anything has to be easier than that experience. I sign the form and am led off to the CT scanner for the planning scan. He offers to follow me up in six weeks but this seems like a waste of both his and my time so I politely decline and say I will be in touch if I have any problems.

I've asked to look at my scan pictures afterwards. I cannot stand the thought of having a scan and not knowing what it shows although the whole purpose of the scan is to line my body up with their equipment so they can zap the correct bit of me. I lie on the table undressed and am lined up with the lasers. I am then scanned. This is my fourth CT. The radiotherapists come back in to tattoo me. Tiny black marks are made over my anterior superior iliac spines bilaterally and in the midline. All done. They let me scroll through the scan images myself. The image quality is a little grainy and there are no coronal views but I can see my left kidney looks moderately hydronephrotic with loss of cortical thickness as before and the adnexal masses maybe look slightly bigger to my untrained eye although I cannot compare them to my previous scan. Oh well, at least I don't feel too bad in myself and hopefully this treatment will fix my bone pain.

I return the following Wednesday for the actual zapping. The waiting room is full of very frail looking elderly people. I wonder how often the 'do nothing' approach is properly explained and offered to these patients. The girls are very punctual. I am soon positioned on the table and my tattoos lined up with the lasers. The treatment takes about five minutes. The machine irradiates me anteriorly first then posteriorly. I wonder if it has to make a noise in order to produce X-rays or if the noise is to make everyone aware that a treatment is in progress. I don't feel any difference immediately. That evening however I feel as though my entire life force has been drained and I cannot seem to get off the sofa. My pain flares up that night. They told me it might and I am prepared with my stockpile of Oxynorm. I skive off work the following day; impressively this is my first day off sick since going back.

41

Changing attitudes

I had no idea that *The Other Side* would have such a massive impact or that so many people would be interested in my little tale. It really was just one lonely scared frustrated girl expressing her emotions about a truly devastating situation. At work today I observe one of my bosses, who has just finished reading the book, sitting down next to a patient on the ward round, holding their hand and properly explaining what the proposed MRI scan will involve in much more detail than he usually would. I flatter myself that perhaps this change in behaviour was down to my literary musings.

I have been receiving numerous messages from other doctors and nurses explaining how the book has changed them. The GPs as a group have been particularly reflective. A Renal Registrar wrote to me vowing never to order another scan without first speaking to the patient and how he now appreciated how difficult a life with nephrostomies must be; something he had not even considered before. Many other doctors have told me how getting communication right especially in the context of breaking bad news is really highlighted in the book and that they have learned much about this important aspect of care from my writing. A final year medical student said she had learned more about communication and always putting the patient first from reading the book than from her five years at medical school. It is amazing to think that I have had this effect on people. We could all as healthcare professionals do to be a little more patient-centred at times and I hope *The Other Side* reminds us of this. It is all too easy for the patient to be lost amongst all the politics, systems and management, but at the end of the day patients should be at the centre of everything we do. These days I remind myself of this fact every time I set foot onto a ward or whenever I start to feel annoyed by the system.

In terms of the impact on me personally as a doctor I definitely do some things differently now when compared with before my illness. In addition to empathy, advocacy and making more time to communicate with patients and their families that I have already discussed I am now much more interested in my patient's lives as individuals. I am in the enviable position of not being that pressurised time-wise and can take my work at a relatively sedate pace so I like to get to know those little details about the people I am looking after that make them special like how long they have been married, what they did for employment, how many grandchildren they have, where they have travelled and so on. I also understand how scary it is to be laid in the hospital bed now so I really try hard to be the friendliest, most approachable doctor that I can be and really focus on the behaviours that I call 'the little things' such as holding a patient's hand when then are upset and making sure I always sit or crouch down next to someone rather than standing over them. DtM is great at 'the little things' and I have learnt a great deal from his bedside manner.

A good death

I have been breaking the unwritten rules of doctoring since I came back to work and have been getting far too emotionally involved. I just cannot help myself. I have such a different outlook on Palliative Care these days and feel facilitating good quality care at the end of life is now probably one of the most important aspects of my professional role. My patients on the LCP have been receiving three or four reviews a day from myself when I am at work and I am determined that I do my very best to achieve symptom control and comfort for these patients and that I offer as much emotional support to their families as I can muster. There is only one opportunity to get it right in this situation and getting it wrong can cause immense lasting harm. The attitude that once a patient is put on the LCP that doctoring seems to stop and all these patients can then expect is a cursory review once a day by the most junior member of the team really frustrates me although I must say many teams in the hospital are doing a fantastic job providing good quality Palliative Care. Nursing staff need support to deliver the 'minute to minute' care and I really feel doctors can have a massive positive impact in these circumstances. It is really is as simple as being 'seen to care'.

I know I shouldn't have favourite patients but I do. Unfortunately my current favourite patient who I have been looking after for ages has been deteriorating clinically. I had sat down with her family and explained what we were hoping to achieve with our treatments a number of weeks ago. I do not erase all hope of survival but her daughter asks me if I think her Mum will leave the hospital. In my heart of hearts I cannot answer this question in the affirmative as her illness trajectory has definitely been on the downward spiral. They are all devastated by my opinion, but grateful for my honesty.

In a way now she has entered the terminal phase of life it is easier as the ground has already been prepared on a communication front. They are all still in such a mess emotionally though. Her husband is falling apart in front of my eyes and it is horrible to watch. They have been married for forty nine years; he cannot remember what life was like without her. She has shown some minimal signs of agitation and pain which have responded well to my usual syringe driver concoction of diamorphine and midazolam. Her daughter is so stressed and agitated I think she would benefit from some benzodiazepines too. We do manage to achieve a peaceful, comfortable death with a well informed, supported family though. No-one can really measure this in their quality indicators but that family were so touchingly thankful for our efforts I will never forget them. They revisit the ward a couple of weeks later. I think there is sometimes a tendency for doctors to avoid relatives after patients have died, maybe something to do with a sense of failure. I however view a peaceful, non-medicalised death as a great success and it is lovely to see them again in a much more settled state emotionally.

Reluctant celebrity

Sheila, the Yorkshire Cancer Centre Director has organised an interview with a local newspaper. She seems well impressed with the thousands of pounds that are pouring her way. I am incredibly nervous about this first interview. I've never really had anything to do with journalists before and Chris comes with me for moral support. She is absolutely lovely though and it is very easy to talk to her about what has happened to me. Shorthand must be a difficult skill to master. I do my first photo shoot at work. I never liked having my photo taken before illness but I am even more self conscious of how I look now. The photographer is very friendly though and it is quite fun doing action shots walking down the ward with some of the nurses. The following week we are surprised to see a photo of Chris and me staring back at us from the front page of the Yorkshire Evening Post with a full page feature on page 3. Despite my new status as a page 3 girl, I am fully clothed! The following day a lady comes up to me in the supermarket, "are you that girl from the paper?" I am a little overcome by being accosted by a complete stranger as I'm trying to think about what to make for tea and nod. "I think you're absolutely marvellous!" I blush.

Marketing appears to me to really just be commonsense although I know people spend years studying how to do it properly at University. The Doctors.net and Facebook hype has died down a little so on a rare quiet day at home I set about bombarding the medical profession and Universities with information about the book. The GP magazines are keen as are the Palliative Care clan and all publish plugs. The medical schools are also very receptive to the idea and many of them post information on their intranet pages about the project. A short letter I have written to the BMA news is also published. I start a scrapbook for all my press cuttings.

People have been demanding an eBook version for ages and I had been resisting obliging these requests. I'm really old fashioned and personally think a book should be an actual thing that you hold and turn the pages of. Books have their own smell, character and history. For these reasons I have never felt the urge to go and buy a Kindle despite loving to read. I eventually give in to public demand though and Chris does the technological bit for me, I wouldn't have known where to start. It is very surreal seeing my book on Amazon and soon there are several five star reviews. Recommendations for the book are popping up all over the Internet.

It's really strange how one thing leads to another with publicity. Another local paper does an interview. Another photo shoot at work. The fan mail has started to pour in too and I'm receiving lots of emails and cards. I feel as though I should reply personally to most of these messages as people have taken the time to write to me often sharing really very personal information about themselves or their family members. It seems rude not to write back and I don't want to use a generic response; that seems wrong to me when people have made such an effort. I'm getting a little bit tired of everyone telling me how brave and inspirational they think I am though. No I'm really not that special, I'm just me ploughing on with my life the only way I know how.

Although I am secretly quite enjoying the limelight, today we have a taste of how intrusive the press can be. It is a Sunday afternoon and we have just returned from a night away at the seaside. I am upstairs writing when the door bell rings. Chris answers it. I listen in as we are not expecting any visitors. It's a journalist who works for a tabloid news agency. He makes out initially that he is linked somehow to the Yorkshire Evening Post and that he was just passing, but Chris luckily doesn't buy this. Who is just passing our house on a Sunday afternoon that is situated on an estate with only one road in and out? This agency had been in touch before trying to get my contact details from the journalist at the YEP and they had messaged me on Facebook. I was reluctant then because I did not want to end up being tabloid fodder. Perhaps it was a little intellectual snobbery creeping in but I really didn't want my story to be misinterpreted by the Red Tops and it to become all about criticising the NHS. That was never the point of me writing the book. He is quite persistent but not many people would get past Chris. I feel my privacy has really been invaded and I'm worried about how he got our address. However after thinking about it I guess he must have accessed the electoral role or something like that. I suppose I should be flattered they are so interested in my story, but the debacle has quite the opposite effect to the one this journalist intended. It has made me even more determined not to speak to them now.

Dark nights

Night-times are long and lonely at the moment. I have a bedtime routine which involves a nice hot bubble bath, Paracetamol, heated wheat pillow and the radio. Falling asleep is not a problem with this relaxing routine but I often wake in the early hours with annoying pelvic pain as my Paracetamol wears off. The pain is not especially severe but it is intrusive and stops me slipping back into peaceful sleep. It feels just like a period but without the accompanying bleeding. I will reheat my wheat pillow and try to get comfy again. Sometimes I give in to taking Oxynorm. I know all my tossing and turning in the middle of the night is disturbing Chris's sleep too, something I feel very guilty about. I will sometimes give up and retire to the sofa or our spare bed so as not to disturb Chris and with the hope that a change of environment will induce sleep but it rarely does. I therefore use this awake time during the night to write or do my embroidery. I also seem to have found a few buddies who share in the insomnia that I email during the night.

It is during these long nights that I have time to contemplate what is happening to me. As I said before I've never felt angry about the situation and I feel strongly that anger would not be a productive emotion in the circumstances so am determined not to let myself feel this way. I guess this is just how my life was meant to be. I do however think that by staying active and positive that I will probably live well for longer than if I retire into a corner with a doom and gloom approach. I get so frustrated when people around me whinge about the least little thing. I think to myself if I can keep smiling in my situation why can't you?

As the weeks have gone by and my symptoms have worsened gradually the feeling of living on borrowed time has been strengthening. For this reason I am so determined not to waste a precious second and I am very aware that my behaviour has become a touch on the hypo-manic side. Perhaps this is contributing to my insomnia. Death is constantly lingering over me and everything that I do. It's so difficult though as no-one can predict what is going to happen or how long I have left. I could die of a PE tomorrow or it could be many months away yet. I do not cope well with this uncertainty and these thought processes dominate my mind during the night.

A rock and a hard place

It's a Monday morning sarcoma clinic again. Six weeks have flown by. Chris comes with me; I need a body guard these days in view of my new found celebrity status! The traffic is awful. Amazingly DtM is on time for once. I am a bit apprehensive about his opinion of *The Other Side* but he keeps most of his thoughts to himself describing it as "good fun". I'm not sure I would describe the experience of being flogged with his poisons 'fun' but there you go. Apparently the book is the talk of Bexley Wing. It was never my intention to offend anyone, just to write an observation of my care and my feelings about illness.

"Let's get down to business". We talk about my symptoms. I play down how bad my pain is, partly because Chris is with me and partly because I don't like whinging. Maybe my mind plays tricks sometimes causing me to somatise. The pain is not stopping me from living my life, but sometimes I wish I could get a proper restful nights sleep. I was such a good sleeper before illness, but the cancer seems to have taken away my ability to and my need for sleep. Recently in addition to my pelvic pain I have been having episodes of right sided flank pain, exactly the same pain as when I was obstructed. It is really worrying me. I am probably being totally illogical as I know my creatinine has remained normal but I really don't want to think about going back to a life with nephrostomies. It sounds defeatist but I think I'd rather die than go through all that again. Slipping into a quiet coma as a consequence of renal failure might not be such a bad way to go. DtM reckons the pain probably relates to my ureteric stents which seems sensible as I will no doubt have an element of vesico-ureteric reflux and ureteric spasm. I have also developed a new problem with a small joint symmetrical inflammatory type arthralgia. I wasn't aware that this can be a late complication of chemotherapy before, but I've done my research about it now. I've also asked a

Rheumatology buddy at work. I'm struggling to write and do procedures in the mornings with the pain and stiffness in my hands and it's at least 10am before it starts to subside. Unfortunately treatment options are limited. DMARDs are really not a good idea in active malignancy, NSAIDs make my haematuria worse and steroids turn me into a psycho bitch. Nothing is ever simple and I guess I will just have to put up with it. I've dealt with much worse symptoms over recent months.

I've had a bad night so I'm feeling pretty sore today. DtM is his usual gentle self as he palpates my abdomen but I am really quite tender on examination. I try to wear my brave face, but I don't think I'd win any poker games. He can't feel any masses but does seems concerned about my lack of adequate analgesia and asks me for my professional opinion whether I would be happy with one of my patients being in so much pain. I suppose I wouldn't but it's such a difficult balancing act and surely it is up to me how much pain I am prepared to tolerate. Of course it's going to be worse when he is poking and prodding me.

I've tried weak opiates such as codeine and tramadol. They don't fix the pain, make me feel spaced out and constipate me so what's the point? Long acting stronger opiates do treat the pain effectively but make me so mentally cloudy that multi-tasking, communicating sensitively and complex decision making at work would be impossible. I didn't mind my brain feeling foggy when I was spending my life lying in a hospital bed being tortured, but now I'm so active and busy I need my mental clarity more than ever. NSAIDs are out of the question with the bladder issues so I'm left with Paracetamol and PRN Oxynorm. The radiotherapy has definitely helped my bone pain, but that isn't really an option for my pelvic masses. He suggests fentanyl patches but I'm sure they will have a similar side effect profile and in a way would be worse as the drug would be delivered all the time instead of just at night which is when I need it really. I tell him I'll think about the patches, more to shut him up than anything else, I probably won't be trying them. I'm determined to retain control of the controllable for as long as possible, and if I can tolerate living with some pain, with the trade-off being retaining my mental clarity then that's what I'm going to do. I'm such a stubborn cow.

We sit and talk quietly in the examination room. I'm sure Chris will be eavesdropping and I'm not entirely sure why DtM does not seem to want to include him in the conversation. Perhaps he thinks it will be easier for me to talk openly without Chris at my side. If this is the case he's probably right. My opinions about further scans and more treatment are elucidated. I think DtM can completely see that I'm not ready for anymore torture just at the moment and he doesn't push it, which pleases me. I'm not sure I'll ever be ready for anymore chemotherapy, but I don't know what problems I'm going to run into in the future and I don't want to burn any bridges with Oncology just yet. "I just don't know", DtM replies "you don't need to know at the moment." I am very clear in my mind that I do not want to be rescanned just for the sake of it.

I have really been feeling external pressures from some family members and friends to consider more chemotherapy recently. The trouble is that some of them do not truly understand the rationale behind palliative treatment and think it's all about prolonging my life so they can have me around for a little bit longer. I have tried to explain the quality of life argument several times but I think it falls on deaf ears. We decide to X-ray my hands and wrists and check my rheumatoid factor and autoantibody screen in view of the arthralgia. I'm sure all the medical chat is going right over Chris's head; I'd better do some explaining later. Another appointment is made for a few weeks time. In the meantime I need to concentrate on staying well and out of hospital.

Soul mates

Our top Bucket List event comes round a few days later. I am like a kid at Christmas and cannot sleep the night before due to excitement instead of pain predominantly. We booked the Renewal of Wedding Vows party about three months ago and to be honest I was not really expecting to be as well as I am for it. I feel extremely lucky to be able to marry the man of my dreams for a second time and the wedding planning has been so much fun. We have written the ceremony ourselves and my close friend Gemma has agreed to officiate for us. I know reading our vows to each other is going to be extremely emotional. We have been practising and haven't managed it without crying yet.

I start the day with the girlies and a thoroughly unhealthy cooked breakfast. We then visit the hairdressers; it has been a long nine months since I have been. My hair has grown back to some extent and everyone keeps telling me how cute I look, but I still do not like the way I look now. I just want my hair back, but I suppose it is a lot quicker to manage these days. I stopped wearing a hat about three weeks ago, this was a big struggle at first but I have persisted and it has become easier. I think I was hiding myself a little bit under my hats, maybe a sign that I am still a little bit unexplainably ashamed about my illness. The hairdresser does a cracking job and I am quite pleased with the results. I do feel a bit silly walking down the high street in my jeans with a sparkly headband in though! Nails next, and I am excited to discover they have nail polish that matches my dress colour almost exactly. My nails have just about regrown after falling off as a result of the chemotherapy.

We arrive at the venue and check into our room. The Buck's Fizz is flowing freely and girls help me to get ready. They have all been so fantastic throughout my illness, not one of them has ever cried on me. They all look gorgeous in their pretty dresses. My brother and his girlfriend pop in as do some of my University friends. It really feels just as exciting as the build up to our original wedding. Sarah helps me into my dress, Kathryn does my make-up and at 3pm we walk round to the room where the ceremony is being held.

A string duet play 'The Arrival of the Queen of Sheba' as we walk in just like at our original wedding. Spontaneous applause occurs. I try to maintain some semblance of bridal serenity. Chris looks so dapper in his smart new suit. Gemma does an amazing job officiating the service and all is going well until we get to the vows. Chris had decided he wanted to go first. It takes him three attempts to get through them and I'm not sure there is a dry eye in the house, even my Mum who never cries is blubbing. We had put a pocket sized packet of tissues on everyone's seats as a joke, but it turns out they come in very handy. I manage to read my vows with a little more composure than Chris; I did not want to ruin my make-up. Black streaks of mascara running down my face would not have been a good look for the photos.

The weather is kind to us for photographs outside and soon Chris and I develop face ache from all the smiling. It is so special to see everyone that is important to us in one place though. The dinner and party are amazing fun; I get a little bit tipsy and spend most of the night in the centre of the dance floor. Chris tells me off for not talking to people more, but I'm having such a good time bopping I don't want to interrupt that. It has been such a long time since me and the girls all had a good dance together. It is 1am when we finally retire to bed. I had a truly wonderful and remarkable day, and am so glad we were able to arrange it so successfully. Just for one night it felt like we stuck two fingers up to the big C. The following morning Chris is a bear with a very sore head. He had been caning the sambuca shots pretty hard. He jokes "you just don't understand the pain I'm in!"

Heroic?

Why as a cancer patient are you seen as 'heroic' and a 'fighter' if you accept all the burdensome, in the most part futile treatment for incurable cancer? Does this mean that if you refuse these interventions that you are somehow foolish or weak? I have been thinking about this a great deal recently. There is a tendency for media surrounding cancer to use highly emotive language. For example the Cancer Research charity slogan is 'together we will beat cancer'. No we won't and I very much doubt DtM is ever going to be out of work. It is a result of being a living organism that cell division and repair will sometimes go awry and the result of this will be cancer. We may become increasingly capable of counteracting the pathology, but I cannot imagine there will ever be a human society without cancer. I do not mean to say that people who choose to go through lots of treatment are doing anything wrong if this is truly what they want to do, but I think all too often patients feel under external pressures to battle on when deep down inside they just want to enjoy their remaining time without so many medical interventions. Death and dying are such taboo subjects in our society and I have never fully understood why, after all it is the one thing that we all have in common, we are all going to die one day. There are campaigns and organisations out there such as 'Dying Matters' and the National Council for Palliative Care tackling these issues but it is going to take such a monumental effort to change societal attitudes. Acceptance is a hugely difficult thing.

I think we could all do to open up discussion with our loved ones about death. I see it all too often when I sit down with families when their relatives are gravely ill that no-one has ever discussed topics such as resuscitation when they were well. I am extremely, perhaps abnormally open about these issues and am completely comfortable talking about them. I realise many people would not be as at ease discussing such things but if just a little of my attitude was adopted I am sure that many of the communication nightmares towards the end of life would be dissipated. Being in the situation I am in I am astonished that more patients with life limiting illnesses do not make their wishes known. Perhaps it is to do with denial. Choosing to talk about resuscitation with a patient on their death bed when they have been battling cancer for months or years is far from the right time in my eyes and these conversations need to happen much earlier in illness. Decisions can always be reviewed, but we all need to be more open and more realistic. I am not saying everyone needs to get down to the solicitors and start making Advance Directives but if we all just asked ourselves 'what would I want if I was dying?' and talked about our answers to that question with our loved ones then I am sure more people would have better deaths.

I didn't view my decision to discontinue chemotherapy in January as particularly brave or on the other hand foolish. I have never regretted making this decision for a single moment. I know some people around me saw it as 'giving up'. I never viewed it as such. I did my best, but the burdens began to outweigh the benefits so I stopped. We will never know if this decision would have had a negative impact on my length of survival but I was suffering so much as a consequence of treatment I could not continue with it. I think I was probably really quite depressed and maybe even slightly delirious. Now I have had a few months to recuperate and live again I probably would consider more treatment when the time comes, but hopefully I can make this decision in the light of all the available information and be able to choose the least burdensome option for me in terms of my quality of life. I would have to be clear that the intent of treatment would be to improve this quality of life, for example to treat pain or other symptoms, rather than just to buy me a few extra weeks of miserable living.

Radio star

"This is crazy, what are we doing?" I ask Chris as we enter the BBC building in Leeds. I have somehow managed to be invited on the One on One show on Radio Leeds. It is a bit like a local version of Desert Island Discs and they have asked me to choose ten of my favourite songs and fill in an extensive questionnaire about myself in preparation for the show. The receptionist is expecting us and we are asked to wait in the reception area. There are television screens looking in on the Look North and Radio Leeds studios. Soon after we arrive so do Ed Balls and Yvette Cooper, our local MPs. It is the day after the local elections so I guess they must be here for that. I have to try hard to restrain Chris from spitting on them. He is not a fan. Neither am I.

At about ten to two the assistant comes to fetch us and take us upstairs. Oh my god. I enter the studio and meet the lady who is going to interview me. They sit me slap bang in front of a large red microphone and after the news headlines the big red 'On Air' light comes on and off we go. There is no preparation about what not to say or what questions are going to be asked. She gives a long introductory spiel about my story and I feel embarrassed. There is a little quiver in my voice as I start to speak but I soon settle down and get into the swing of it. She asks me some quite tough questions especially around my feelings about illness. Towards the end of the show she asks Chris to come in. I had managed to maintain my composure so far but he sets off my tears when he is asked to explain what I mean to him. It was a great experience and I am buzzing afterwards. I want to do it again. My confidence must be back. We listen to the CD of the show in the car on the way home. I cringe a bit, but at least I got two of my three challenge words into the interview. These were inconsequential, procrastinate and quagmire. I didn't manage to succeed with quagmire! The feedback is that I have had everyone in tears and that I came across as composed and articulate. I'm really not sure I agree with these comments after listening myself and found it all a little bit cringe worthy.

The ancient art of sticking pins in

I have been keen to try some non-pharmacological strategies for pain control. Several options have been crossing my mind, but I decide to go with acupuncture. I think it is probably the one complementary therapy with a reasonably sound evidence base and I was successfully treated with acupuncture many years ago for troublesome migraine. The Oncologists will probably think it is all 'clap trap', but I have a very open mind for a Western medic and am willing to try any opiate avoiding strategies I can think of. There must be a sound foundation to it or people wouldn't have used it for thousands of years would they?

My therapist is a lovely girl about my age. She takes a full medical history and approaches it almost exactly as I would. She follows the SOCRATES method for a pain history and is probably more thorough than most FY1 doctors. I hop up on her couch and she sticks the needles in my feet, legs, hands, abdomen, head and ears. They do not hurt at all; in fact I cannot even feel most of them going in. I suppose I have had to contend with much larger scarier needles over recent months. A strange tingly sensation occurs after they are inserted. She leaves me in a darkened room with peaceful music playing for half an hour. I think I doze off.

I return the following week for another session. It is difficult to be objective about whether the treatment has helped or not although I think I have been sleeping a bit better and have used a little less Oxynorm during the night. It is however a very relaxing peaceful experience whether it helps my symptoms or not and I need all the help I can get to stay stress free, calm and cheerful at the moment. It would be all too easy to slip into black dog mode given the circumstances, but I am determined to avoid this happening. I continue to attend for treatment each week.

Making friends

During the first phase of my illness I was very isolated from other patients and didn't really feel the need to connect with others suffering similar experiences in those early months. I was quite happy living the nightmare in relative seclusion with my family, close friends and a few colleagues as my support network. I never really felt I fit into a particular patient group when I was in hospital. I was too long in the tooth to fit into the teenager group, but was too young to fit into the older patient group either. I think the 'thirty somethings' have perhaps become a lost tribe within the NHS. The Teenage Cancer Trust has done great work making life better for teenagers and people in their early twenties. There are different challenges for those of us in our thirties though. Although it does not affect me, a lot of patients my age are struggling with the combination of life limiting illness and a young family or grappling with fertility issues. There are also probably more financial burdens to face such as mortgages and the effects of illness on careers.

I have however over time begun to make friends as a result of my illness. Through my research on DSRCT I stumbled across the online forum and Facebook groups for sufferers. These are exclusive clubs that I'm not sure anyone would want the credentials to become a member of, but the mutual support of others going through the same experiences is comforting. Some of the members are incredibly knowledgeable. It is nice to be able to offer support and advice to others starting out on the treatment pathway such as which anti-emetics work during chemotherapy. The Americans are so aggressive with their attitude towards treating this disease though. Some people have been on the P6 protocol for nearly two years. How on earth could they put themselves through that? Someone posted that they were scared to discontinue treatment for fear of recurrence. They all seem obsessed with having multiple operations, getting accepted into clinical trials and achieving 'No Evidence of Disease' status. The possibility of surgery did cross my mind at one point, but I soon accepted that I was not a surgical candidate and that I did not want to spend the final months of my life recovering from a laparotomy anyway. I seem to have the polar opposite attitude towards my own treatment compared to most on the forum in that one of my aims is to have as few hospital interventions as possible to maintain my quality of life. There is absolutely no point striving for a cure when that is never going to be realistically achievable.

One lady whose son died from DSRCT a number of years ago has regularly been in touch with me via email. She is a midwife in Manchester and is amazingly supportive. I try to keep her updated with my activities. I have also developed a few email buddies from the 'Doctors as Patients' forum on Doctors.net. It is nice to share experiences of the frustrations and challenges surrounding being a member of the profession whilst simultaneously needing to use health services as a patient.

Argumentative

It is the 6th June. As I update our patient list on the computer with the date prior to the ward round it suddenly hits me that I really did not expect to still be here. I definitely did not expect to still be physically reasonably well and working. I have even had to buy myself a new academic diary. I did not think I would outlive my old one but seemingly I am going to. I hope this is not tempting fate.

I have always had a great deal of respect for the Consultant doing today's round and she has taught me an awful lot over the past couple of years. The ward manager also joins us; she is an absolutely fantastic nurse. The first patient is very functionally dependant following a stroke and has been admitted with general deterioration secondary to a bout of pneumonia. His overall condition has declined including his swallowing which is no longer safe. We have been forced to feed him via a nasogastric tube which has been traumatic as he has still managed to pull three tubes out despite a nasal bridle and mittens. It is a distressing situation. He doesn't have any family and we are involving an IMCA to help make healthcare decisions in his best interests, particularly whether a PEG would be appropriate. Hopefully his swallow will recover, but in reality it may not. His care home have told us that he has previously said that he would not want tube feeding, but unfortunately there is no advance directive to validate this. He is not really communicating enough to explore his wishes.

The case emphasises to me my need to clarify my Preferred Priorities for Care and make the important people in my life aware of them. I do not ever want to go to ICU, although I'm absolutely sure no sensible Intensivist would ever have me. If I develop another obstructive uropathy I would like a sensible discussion about what to do about this and not to just be automatically sent off to the torture chamber for a nephrostomy without any consideration whether it is the right thing to do or not. If I am delirious and unable to partake in this discussion myself then I want Chris and my parents to be consulted about my best interests. And I never ever under any circumstances want to be resuscitated.

The next patient is a lady in her 80s from a nursing home. She has presented with a general decline over the past few weeks and has gone from being able to transfer with two people to being hoisted. She has an underlying dementia. Someone has requested a head CT which has shown a probable tumour. The boss initially wants to repeat the CT with contrast and even talks about an MRI. I however see things differently these days. The Neurosurgeons are never going to touch this lady with a barge pole given her age and pre-morbid level of dependency so why are we worrying about the diagnosis? It is completely academic. Scanning the patient again will probably cause her a great deal of distress for what purpose exactly? Let's pop her on some steroids, make sure she has adequate analgesia and get her home. I voice my opinion and my viewpoint is adopted. There are never any right answers in cases like these but sometimes it is best to pursue a pragmatic approach.

We then see a 98 year old patient who had suffered an intra-cerebral haemorrhage some weeks ago. His condition has been relatively static for a number of weeks and there has been an ongoing debate about whether a PEG would be appropriate. The general feeling amongst the Stroke Consultants is that we should proceed with a PEG, the nutrition team do not agree and the family are a little divided on the issue. Personally I feel quite strongly that a PEG is not in this chap's best interests. His swallow is not completely unsafe although his oral intake is variable, he is extremely frail and I feel the quoted procedure related mortality of 1% is probably a massive underestimation in his case. First do no harm. I very rarely disagree with this Consultant on clinical decisions. The ward manager agrees with me on the issue and together we conduct the best interests meeting that afternoon with the nutrition specialist nurse. Luckily his children have been discussing things amongst themselves and have decided that they do not feel their Dad would have wanted a PEG and that we should proceed with discharge planning to a care home. The meeting is much more straightforward than we had anticipated. The ethical dilemmas surrounding artificial nutrition are and always will be a proper minefield.

Living with it

I'm not sure what the etiquette is for living life with a terminal cancer diagnosis hanging over you. I guess there is no rule book for a situation like this and I am very much of the opinion that I can only do my very best to plough on with things and try to be as normal and active as possible for as long as possible, bearing in mind that I might feel rubbish and that things may start to get on top of me both physically and psychologically at times. I am therefore packing as many activities into my life as is humanly possible. If someone asks me to do something these days and I'm free then I say yes with no hesitation. I have quite high expectations of what I can achieve in my remaining time; some might feel these expectations are set too high. I have always been an ambitious individual though and this aspect of my character is not going to change just because I am dying.

At work I seem to be attempting to fit in what I used to do in five days into only three. Even though I am not doing quite as much clinically each week I still seem to have just as many non-clinical commitments on my plate, perhaps even more. I have decided that building my own CV is a little pointless now and have stopped doing my own ePortfolio but am busy CV building for all the junior doctors working with me. I was slightly obsessive about my ePortfolio before illness, but I guess life is too short to worry it now. I have set up an audit project from scratch on the neurosurgical management of subdural haematomas and I am extremely busy with teaching. I know my story is becoming more common knowledge and I wonder what the students think of me. I'm sure some of them will have read the book. I have managed to infiltrate some Elderly Care topics into the FY1 shadowing teaching programme including 'recognition and management of the dying patient'. My plan is to indoctrinate them early into the idea of providing good quality Palliative Care in the hospital setting. Several of the newbie doctors comment this is a topic that has not been taught about much before at Medical School although it is a common scenario that they will have to deal with from day one in August. They seem grateful for my efforts. The End of Life Strategy group is also keeping me busy and I have taken on some projects for this including analysing complaints made about end of life care and rolling out the use of Preferred Priorities for Care within the Elderly Medicine Department. Hopefully through this work I can improve Palliative Care in the hospital.

At home I am not content unless there are at least three enjoyable things in the diary each week and regularly there are far more than this. I really appreciate the simple things in life now and just having dinner with good friends, baking a cake or going for a nice walk in the countryside make me happy. I know there will come a point where I will need to slow down but we have not reached this point yet and I keep going. Several old friends have recently been in touch and it is so lovely finding out what everyone is up to now. I have arranged to meet up with some of them. The mundane stuff in life also still needs to be done and although family members keep offering to help with the laundry or the housework I am very keen that as long as I am physically able to do it I will. It is my wifely duty to make sure my husband has clean ironed shirts to wear for work and that duty doesn't disappear just because I'm dying of cancer. 'Being normal for as long as possible' is the mantra I am sticking to at the moment.

I just don't know anymore

Although I do not want to admit it to myself, to Chris or the family my health has been noticeably deteriorating over recent weeks. The pain is definitely worsening, my energy levels are waning and I think I can palpate a mass in my abdomen again. Sleep has also been more elusive than usual. I have been doing my best to maintain a brave face but the last few days I have failed and ploughing on is becoming increasingly difficult. I am struggling to stand up for an entire ward round and I have to sit down at every opportunity. I have ended up going home early on several occasions due to uncontrolled pain and unusually for me have had some days off sick. I do not really know what I want to do about it. DtM had suggested a deterioration in my quality of life would be an indication to consider more treatment. I am not entirely sure whether what I am currently experiencing constitutes the sort of deterioration he meant though. Quality of life is such a subjective concept. The thought of more chemotherapy however still fills me with terror, a word I do not use lightly. I have been starting to research what second line treatment options would entail though. I need to be well informed to come to a sensible decision.

I have finally given in to strong opiates again and am back on a small dose of Oxycontin at night. The hangover effect in the morning is noticeable but not too bad and I don't think it is affecting my work too much. I am all too aware that my personality is dampened and my thought processes are slowed as result of the drugs though and I have to be more careful with my decision making at work. I cannot help but feel a sense of failure by having to resort to the hardcore drugs again, no matter how many people tell me how irrational this feeling is. I know deep down inside they are just tools to help me cope, but I still feel as though I have somehow failed. For these reasons I know I am being too conservative with my dose.

My brother and his girlfriend have just announced their engagement. I cannot explain how excited and happy I am about this news. Beth is a truly lovely girl who is so good for Adam and we really enjoy her company, she is such good fun. I am very close to my brother and knowing that he will be settled in life before I pop my clogs is comforting. I have spent most of my adult life worrying about him. They have fixed a date in only ten weeks time. Perhaps self-centredly I initially think the rush to the forthcoming nuptials might have been something to do with them wanting me to be able to attend the wedding, but when we see Beth she is glowing and is obviously in the family way. All I can think is 'wow'. Then to add to my excitement a little more they ask me to be a bridesmaid, something I have never done before. I am unusual amongst my close friends to be the married one.

All this fantastic news is a little bittersweet though especially in the context of my recent deterioration in health. If DtM had asked me to consider more chemotherapy in January I probably would have said "no, never again thank you very much, get lost and leave me alone." However this change in my personal circumstances has got me thinking would I take some more suffering in an attempt to stick around a little longer and meet my new niece or nephew? My outlook seems to have changed with the situation and I just don't know what to think anymore. I retreat into quiet contemplation; I can see Chris is really worried about me.

It feels like everyone else's lives around me are just getting started as mine is coming to an end. There is of course Adam and Beth's wonderful news, but also my friend Sarah has just bought a house with her boyfriend and two of my other special friends Kathryn and Gemma are becoming settled in long-term relationships. My friend Effie has just invited us to her wedding in October and Lizzy, my best friend from University has just passed all her GP exams and landed herself the perfect first proper job. The junior doctors I have been mentoring for their PACES exams have all been successful too.

It's very strange and difficult to deal with my emotions about good news now. I want to be and am genuinely happy for people around me and I completely realise that life has to go on. I really want it to and I cannot stand the thought of everyone moping about for weeks on end grief stricken when I do die. But there is always this undertone in my mind that I am going to miss out on seeing everyone else's lives flourish.

One of Chris's friend's Mums has just died from ovarian cancer. She was being looked after by the first Oncologist I ever saw and was on my old ward in the Bexley Wing. I am really upset by this news even though I have never even met her. I suppose selfishly it brings it home that my own mortality is awaiting me in the relatively near future. Another of Chris's friend's Mums has also just been diagnosed with a likely renal cell carcinoma and is awaiting surgery. I seem to be surrounded by cancer at the moment, which is also clouding my judgement. Perhaps in reality I am not as ready for death as I thought I was despite all my attempts to prepare myself properly for it.

Disheartened

I receive my first negative review of *The Other Side* on Amazon today. Someone has given it 2 stars and commented that they feel I am self indulgent and that I have an over inflated view of my own clinical skills when compared to all the clinicians who have looked after me. I am so upset by this. I am not naïve and completely realise that not everyone who will read the book will enjoy it, and that people are entitled to their own opinion. However, I am really complementary about lots of characters in the book and in real life I have a fairly low opinion of my own skills. In fact I have often been told in 360 degree feedback that I should be more confident in myself.

I am in a fairly vulnerable place emotionally at the moment anyway with everything else that is going on and this episode knocks some of the wind out my sails. Lots of people are quick to jump to my defence. A colleague tells me about the Internet phenomenon of 'trolling', where people go round the Internet posting deliberately inflammatory and derogatory comments in an attempt to provoke a response. Perhaps I have been 'trolled' or perhaps this person did really genuinely feel the book conveyed these traits. I wouldn't mind if they were criticising my writing style since I am certainly no experienced writer, but the comments feel like an attack on my character from someone who does not know me either professionally or personally. A friend tells me the review is "not worth the cyber space it is written in" and "to not waste my precious time ruminating about it". In reality it is going to take an awful lot of positive comments to counteract it though.

Hmmm...

I have knocked off work early to come over to Leeds for my Sarcoma clinic appointment. It has been a frustrating morning. Nothing was where it should be, nobody was answering the phone and I am looking after a few patients at the moment that we are really struggling to sort out clinically. To add to me not being in the best of moods I have been feeling increasingly ill for the past few days. My clinical deterioration is definitely real now and there is no doubt about it. I have had some intermittent PV bleeding and in my eyes this could only really represent disease progression. I am sleep deprived too which is not helping. Perhaps I should take more drugs, but I am walking a fine line between adequate analgesia and functioning at the moment and would rather stick to the functioning side of this line if at all possible. I'm in a 'shrug my shoulders to the world' kind of mood which is unlike me; I'm usually so 'face up to it all' head on.

Sitting in waiting rooms has become an uncomfortable experience these days as I am often recognised and I can tell people are talking about me. I try to distract myself from the attention today by reading an article about illness trajectories in my Palliative Care journal when DtM fetches me. Some might think my choice of reading material a little strange for a terminally ill person, but I still have my original clinical interests and Palliative Care in the acute hospital setting is one of them. He is early! In response to the initial "how are you" question I respond "Hmmm" and after a considered pause, "not so well." Despite some relatively minor problems overall things have been really good health-wise since January until recently, but I guess by not treating an aggressive cancer for five months we were always going to come to this point eventually. I am surprised I have lasted this long if I'm honest with myself. I tell him about the pain, insomnia and bleeding. I also tell him Adam's news. It is easier to admit to and be honest about my symptoms in the absence of Chris. I have kept most of how I am feeling from him recently. He has me on my death bed with the least little twinge. I am subdued and feel rather pathetic. "Are you not feeling up to facing it all today?" No I'm not really but I have to, come on and pull yourself together Kate.

My tummy is really sore on palpation; much more so than at my last clinic visit. My right loin is also tender, an ominous sign. I really hope the stent is still patent. I'm a bit sweaty and cold peripherally. "Are you sicker than you are letting on?" Probably, but don't you dare even think about admitting me. I shrug. "Your abdomen is reminiscent of how it was when we started out." At least I'm not imagining things.

My clinical deterioration seems to constitute his idea of a reduction in my quality of life that would spark a conversation about second line treatment. We talk about the options. He wants to try cisplatin. I ask about the American's regimen with temozolamide and irinotecan. Cisplatin sounds like it is easier to give and less burdensome to have though. We also talk about scans. I have always been clear that there is no point doing a scan if the result is not going to change what we do. This is one of the basic cornerstones of Geriatric Medicine which I try to respect in my own practice. He throws radiotherapy into the mix as a means of symptom control and that it would be useful to understand the anatomy of the tumour for this reason as well as objectively documenting my disease prior to chemotherapy to be able to measure any response to treatment. I guess I'll have to have a scan. It feels like the right thing to do. I'm pleased it will be a CT though and that I do not have to face the tunnel of doom that is the MRI scanner.

Considering chemotherapy sensibly raises a few other questions, the most important of which is my shocking venous access. My veins took quite a pounding in hospital and the veins in the backs of my hands are shot to pieces, they are not even palpable anymore. The one decent vein I have in my right ante-cubital fossa for venepuncture is becoming sclerosed over time and I do not relish the thought of multiple cannulation attempts every time I come in for treatment. "Do you know what the options are for vascular access?" I've got a pretty good idea. I think a Portacath might be the best solution if I am to continue working, but we will have to think about it further in the light of my decision whether to proceed with treatment or not.

"Will we reach a point of no return?" I am very uneasy to hear that he feels a likely mode of death for me is going to be a bowel obstruction, one of my greatest innermost fears. I have always realised this was going to be a possibility given the location of my disease but I think I have been burying my head in the sand about it. If I do develop this chemotherapy will not work quickly enough in his experience to rescue the situation. Hmmm. The thought of TPN, NBM, nasogastric tubes, an ileostomy and puking my guts up at the end fills me with dread. I would much rather die than go through all that and would seriously contemplate suicide should this scenario arise. I have already stockpiled enough appropriate drugs in the house to make sure this would be successful if needed. "I think you have a much lower threshold than the average patient to accept a palliative approach." I suppose I do, but I guess this is true of most doctors. We have seen so much needless suffering in our day to day lives to want to go through it ourselves. In my experience futility is a difficult concept to grasp for lay patients, but as doctors we grapple with this all the time. There was an interesting article about these very points printed in the Guardian earlier this year, 'How doctors choose to die', which I read with great interest.

As I leave he asks "don't get angry with me, but are you sure you are managing your analgesia ok?" Hmmm. Perhaps not, but I am not relinquishing control over this yet. I really felt like DtM had all the time in the world for me this afternoon. It was a proper patient centred consultation and although I now have some difficult decisions to make over the coming days I feel better armed with the information to make them. Our discussion was neither patronising nor above me, never easy to achieve with a medically trained patient. I will of course be consulting Chris, the family and my colleagues about what they think I should do too, but ultimately I guess the decision is mine and I will have to make it. After all I am the one who has to go through the treatment and I can certainly be deemed to have full mental capacity.

My lovely husband and I go out for dinner to our favourite seafood restaurant that evening and mull it over. Of course he wants me to have the chemotherapy. Mum does too. So do my friends and my colleagues. I'm absolutely sure everyone will support me regardless of my decision though. My initial thoughts are that I will probably give it a whirl and at least see how bearable it is. Nothing can be as bad as the last time, can it? At least cisplatin is given as an outpatient and the risk of neutropaenia is low. If I don't try I will probably spend my remaining time wondering what would have been and regretting it. It is an ambition of mine to die with no regrets.

Worries

The usual things that seem to scare people, particularly women about chemotherapy do not bother me that much. Losing my hair was not nice but not particularly traumatic in the whole grand scheme of things. It had to go; it grew back albeit now curly. I liked wearing my hats. Losing my fertility has never really bothered me that much either. It would be completely unrealistic to want to bring a child into this situation. We have always said how glad we are not to have had children before we found out about my illness. It would have been a proper nightmare to have to cope with, especially for Chris and my heart really goes out to people who have to deal with this, it must be horrendous.

The things that bother me most about chemotherapy are the isolation from the world caused by constant hospital stays, coping with the bone marrow failure making you feel so ill you can barely get out of bed, the loss of interest in food and anticipating what is coming as the poisoning begins. I have never suffered with anticipatory nausea but I can completely see how some other patients develop this. Knowing that an infusion is going to make you feel horrendous a few hours later as it trickles into your bloodstream is a really hard psychological barrier to tackle. I have gone off my food a little bit just at the thought of having more chemotherapy. At least I will not have to face the dreaded hospital food this time. I am determined fatigue is not going to get me this time either and I plan to continue working if I can. Surprisingly last time I was not all that fatigued despite everything I went through.

So my main fears and anxieties about chemotherapy may not be a problem with the cisplatin as it is an outpatient regimen and at least some of life should be able to continue without being held hostage in a Bexley Wing side room hopefully. I am not relishing the thought of facing the vomit bowls again though. Cisplatin is a highly emetogenic agent according to DtM and my reading. There is always my trusty Nozinan to hopefully help with this though.

I attend for my CT scan the day after the clinic appointment; I am impressed they have managed to squeeze me onto a list at Leeds General Infirmary so quickly. It is years since I have set foot in this hospital and it is really quite nostalgic walking down the long corridors. I have some very happy memories of working here and really found my feet as a clinician during this time. It's strange how every hospital has its own distinctive smell. One of my Consultant friends has kindly agreed to sit with me whilst I drink the oral contrast; she is currently off work with a broken arm. The hour passes quickly and it is extremely useful to chat through what was said yesterday and how I am feeling about everything. She has a very good pair of ears that perhaps I bend far too often. They take me through. I feel sorry for the CT radiographer on cannulation duties this afternoon. I had blood taken from my best vein yesterday and my other veins are shall we say non-existent. Three very sore attempts later she succeeds. We are going to have to get some vascular access sorted for chemo; I am not particularly needle phobic but I cannot be going through that every single time.

This is my fifth CT scan. I lie on the table and am hooked up to the contrast machine. I am so used to the routine by now. No I am not pregnant. Have you seen my hormone profile? My FSH and LH levels are through the ceiling and anyway getting pregnant would involve having sex, something neither Chris nor I are particularly interested in doing at the moment. The scouting scans are performed and I hold my breath as instructed. The radiographer comments on the presence of my ureteric stents. He is a very good looking chap with a South African accent. The contrast is injected. I flush and experience the incontinence sensation about half way into the infusion. How weird. I haven't experienced this sensation during previous scans; I wonder why not. A couple more passes through the machine and we're done.

Out of hand

The following week an article about me is published in the Daily Mail. I have been working on this for a number of weeks with a freelance journalist who had contacted me at work after seeing the piece in the Yorkshire Evening Post. Her approach was much less intrusive than the News Agency that had been harassing me and I instantly like her 'down to earth' and motherly character. She had the lovely idea of summarising my story into a short diary using extracts from the book and has been reading the article out to me over the phone. We have spent a long time translating the medical jargon into a more easily readable format for the lay audience. The photo shoot takes a long four hours. The photographer is a lovely girl, and although I am becoming experienced at photo shoots now with the previous press coverage I am never going to be confident with it no matter how many times I do it. Anyone who thinks a career in modelling is glamorous is sadly misguided.

Although I trust the journalist I am still quite apprehensive about the actual article, after all no matter how much you have been involved in the editing you never really know what the Press are going to print until you actually see it in black and white. Chris fetches the paper first thing in the morning. It is not difficult to find the article as it is the centre two-page spread. Oh my god. There is a huge picture staring back at me from a national newspaper. The photo looks ok I suppose. The article has been published as we had written it and I am happy with it. The website has lots of the photos I had given them from significant events in our lives. The nice comments are pouring in as are the book orders, after all the whole point of the article was to sell some more books so I guess it has served its purpose.

The following day I am asked to appear on our regional television news programme. Seriously, me on television, this is really getting out of hand. How has my life come to this? If you'd told me I'd be appearing in national newspapers and on television six months ago I probably would have thought you were completely insane and sectioned you! A cameraman comes to the hospital in the afternoon to film some action shots of me with colleagues at work. Everyone on the ward is dead giddy about it and I cannot believe how many people want to be involved.

They send a taxi to take me to the studio like I am somehow important. I would have been happy getting the bus. Chris meets me there. The producer is extremely handsome and amicable. They sit us in the green room and the main presenter comes by for a quick chat before the interview. This is all so surreal, but it has been such a whirlwind that I have not really had the time to comprehend what I am doing and get too nervous about it. Chris is miffed they don't want him to appear too but I am so glad he is with me for some moral support. There is quite a palaver arranging the microphone cables to ensure they are not visible. Everyone is so friendly.

The floor manager takes us through to the studio. It is smaller than I expected it to be and the illusion of the backdrop being a window looking out over Leeds countryside on the television is in reality a video screen. Three cameras are staring at me. I try to ignore them and sit down with the best lady like posture I can manage. Red lights on, finger count down and off we go. It is over before I know it and I have managed it in one take without any stuttering. Not bad for a first attempt. Afterwards they let me sign their studio wall. I choose a spot below John Cleese and above Tony Christie, what a place to be! I cringe from behind a cushion as we watch the interview back later that evening.

The next day a producer from BBC Breakfast gets in touch. They want me to appear on their sofa too. This is properly getting out of hand now. A national TV programme. Little old me, surely nobody is that interested are they? The broadcast journalist who does the research interview informs me they have an average audience of eight million at 7.40am, the slot they have lined up for me with Bill and Suzanna on the following Wednesday. If that doesn't sell some books, I'm not sure what will! Sheila at the YCC is going to be so chuffed that her relatively small charity is going to get such national exposure too. I am definitely in need of a new dress and a haircut in preparation for this appearance.

My Parents

I haven't mentioned my Mum and Dad much in my story telling before but they have been a constant support in my life that I really do not know what I would have done without. There are some nice facets to illness if you look for the silver lining and the creation of time to spend with your family and friends is definitely one of these aspects. A month could go by without seeing my parents before cancer even though they live relatively nearby and I wouldn't even always speak on the phone every week. I would blame this on being busy with work but in reality it was probably just laziness. This has completely changed now and I speak to Mum every couple of days and see them most weeks. I feel very supported and loved by them. Mum shares my black humour about dying and often jokes about 'not needing your inheritance' if she buys me a present. Dad is much quieter about the whole situation but I can see he is proud of me regarding my achievements with *The Other Side* and he has recorded all my media appearances.

I often stay over at their house when Chris is away with work or is going out with his friends. Mum calls it 'baby-sitting'. Being at home is very comforting and I find it relaxing and much easier to switch off there. Mum recently knitted a blanket for their sofa and I love wrapping myself up in it and drifting off after a cheeky glass of wine in the evening. She always says "I didn't so much lose a daughter when you left home but more gain a sofa!" I think I generally sleep a little better at home, although the dawn chorus is deafening being in the countryside. She likes to feed me up and has always been a fantastic cook. It's where my love of food and cooking stems from. I know she hated seeing me pushing my food around my plate when I was ill and used to regularly bring food parcels into the hospital to try and tempt me. Typical mothering behaviour I guess.

They have offered their house for my final weeks if I want to go there. I haven't definitely decided what I would like to do yet, but I know Chris will struggle with looking after me, especially the personal care side of things and if I'm going achieve my wish to stay out of a hospital or hospice environment at the end then going to Mum and Dad's might be the most practical solution. I'm not sure how we would get me up all the steps at the front of their house if I'm really ill though, but I guess we will cross that bridge if and when we come to it. Going home also has the advantage of being in an area where I do not know the local Palliative Care Team. I know the local community Macmillan nurse in Wakefield really well; we have worked together at the hospital for years before she took up a community post. I would not want to see her as a patient and I'm sure she would not want to be involved in my care either.

Mum has often said that they will continue to consider Chris part of the family when I do die. It is lovely to think that he will remain their son-in-law even though I won't be there. We have been so lucky with our respective in-laws and how we both fitted very easily into each other's families with no problems. I am very fond of Chris's family particularly his Grandma and I know my Mum and Dad are fond of Chris.

Turned upside down and inside out

DtM fetches me from the waiting room. It has only been ten days since I saw him last. The recent media frenzy has provided me with some distractions but I'm still a total nervous wreck regarding my CT results. Immediately even before I have chance to sit down he asks how my symptoms are. "About the same, I'm still smiling though". He has got my images up on PACS. There is no formal report yet. I ask to see the coronal views as I find it easier to appreciate anatomy in this format. The scan from December looks the same as the scan from last week. The adnexal masses are about the same size, the left upper quadrant mass is not really that obvious and my liver looks ok. Hmmm. I'm not very good at receiving good news, let's face it I haven't had all that much practice at it during my illness. I had properly psyched myself up to see a scan showing deteriorating disease and to face up to accepting more treatment. I don't really know what to say or do so I sit myself down in the furthest away seat. DtM admits he was expecting to see worsening disease too.

The pertinent question is why am I suffering so much at the moment then if it's not disease progression? I had a terrible night on Saturday. Chris and I went out for dinner to recreate our first ever date in Leeds as part of the Bucket List and I could barely walk back to the hotel I was in so much pain. There then followed a long uncomfortable Oxynorm fuelled night, which has sadly become the norm of late. Perhaps I am imagining it, but I really don't think I am. DtM wants to go over my symptoms again, but I'm not in the mood for repeating myself. I'm not really in the mood for talking full stop. I should be happy; stability off treatment in partially treated DSRCT is not to be expected. I don't however feel very happy right now and I cannot really rationalise how I'm feeling. How weird and pathetic.

He asks about my analgesia regimen at the moment. I reluctantly tell him what I'm taking. I know this will spark a debate I do not particularly wish to become embroiled in about whether I am on high enough or frequent enough doses. I am really struggling to open up today. He comes and sits down next to me. There follows a gentle lecture on the pharmacology of opiates and what he thinks I should do. I listen, play with my scarf and avoid eye contact for the most part. There is no way I am going to work in a hospital and act as the senior member of the junior medical team under the influence of drugs. End of story. And I want to enjoy my time outside of work too without the emotional numbing effect of opiates. I know that his heart is in the right place and he is just trying to help, but I'm not sure I am particularly in the mood to be helped today. Perhaps I am being arrogant or stubborn or just plain difficult. I guess this is the patient's prerogative though.

I agree it may be time to see my Palliative Medicine Consultant again; she will probably have some more clever suggestions. He wants me to repeat an MSU and see me again in two or three weeks. I feel as my disease is stable that seeing me again this soon might be wasting his time. He probably has far more needier patients than me. He doesn't agree and does seem genuinely concerned about my symptom control, which is nice. I very much view him as my poisons man though and thankfully I am not in need of these skills at the moment. He promises to phone once he has discussed my scans with a Radiologist to make sure we are not missing anything subtle.

I email DtM the following day to apologise for being a total nightmare at clinic. Now the news has had time to settle I am feeling much more rational and have allowed myself to feel happy about it. Seeing other people's reactions to my scan results is also helping me to feel grateful about the stay of execution that I have just received. I am perhaps a little less distressed by the pain too as I now know it is not related to cancer progression. The clinician in me would still like a reasonable explanation for it though. I really didn't think I was a somatiser particularly. DtM writes back to say that he wished all his patients were as thoughtful and informed as me and that he finds it easier to look after me than I perceive it to be. That's nice. At least this false start has forced me into thinking what I would do with regards to further treatment in the future. Hopefully this will make it easier when the time does inevitably come round although I may feel differently again in a few months. DtM's clinic letter arrives a few days later; it infers my stubborn attitude during the consultation, but it is written in a very diplomatic way. I smile whilst reading it.

More Bucket List

Chris and I drive up to the Yorkshire Gliding Club at Sutton Bank in North Yorkshire. It's beautiful scenery, but I am constantly looking at the skies wondering whether it is flyable weather. Chris gets stuck into moving the boy's toys about when we arrive and I just watch. The price of illness I guess. All the volunteers are really friendly and the Consultant who is organising the day is like a kid in a sweet shop. He has organised it under the guise of an 'F1 Transitions to Practice' conference, but really I think it is just a chance for him to indoctrinate more people into his new favourite hobby. My FY1 and I present about teaching skills and Chris sees a different side to me that he hasn't seen before standing up in front of people speaking about a topic I'm extremely passionate about.

After a typically stodgy Yorkshire lunch of pie and chips it's time to take to the skies. I am strapped into a parachute and shown how to use it. Jesus I hope I don't need it! Then I gingerly climb into the glider and am strapped in further. They go through the emergency escape procedure with me, there is no chance I would ever manage it in a panic, but dying in a glider crash is probably much better than the mode of death that awaits me so I am not too apprehensive. Dave, my pilot is very reassuring. The tow plane takes off pulling us along the bumpy ground and soon we are airborne. We rapidly climb to two thousand feet and the tow rope is released with quite a jolt. We are on our own now. It is so quiet, but I suppose there is no engine. Even though it is a cloudy day you can still see for miles and the views are awe inspiring. I feel remarkably calm though and manage to make a good video of the landing. The whole experience was incredible and really dare-devil by my standards. I am so glad to have had the opportunity to do it.

We have been praying for some sunshine for the cricket and despite all the weather forecasts earlier in the week suggesting it was going to be a washout God has been kind to us as he often is these days and it is set fair. The trip to the cricket has been arranged by the Ponte Crew and it is lovely to see everyone. Sitting in the sunshine with an ice-cream watching Yorkshire beat the living daylights out of Leicestershire is just the kind of reminiscent experience I hoped it would be. They even bowl them all out on the very last ball of the match. Yes! Bucket List tick.

Our trip to the Zoo was a few weeks ago. I have very fond memories of visits to Chester Zoo when we were kids and I wanted to go again. Adam and Beth come with Mum, Dad and me. Unfortunately Chris is busy with work. We are again lucky with the weather. I'm sure someone up there is looking down kindly on me. The red pandas, possibly my favourite animal in the Zoo are out and about being very active in their trees. I stand and watch for ages. Dad gets some great photographs of the baby elephants. I brave the bat enclosure for the first time ever, but I am petrified as they fly over me and quickly make my exit. Adam and Beth look so in love today and I feel quite content too. It is a perfect day and predictably I fall asleep in the car on the way home. Another Bucket List tick.

Problem solving

DtM emails back a couple of days later to say he has reviewed my CT with the Radiologists and that they feel my symptoms may be related to the left stent being mal-positioned. He asks how I feel about a procedure to sort it out. My knee jerk response is to leave it alone for now. I will need my stents changing in a few months anyway as they should only be in situ for a twelve month period and although I had not originally planned to outlive them; this seems like a distinct possibility now. The thought of procedures and hospitals is not one I really want to contemplate at the moment. I decide to try and stop being so stubborn about analgesia and take a few days out of my hectic punishing schedule to trial some higher doses of opiates to see if I can return to a normal sleep pattern and achieve better symptom control. Unfortunately I have no success.

I email DtM back at 3am a few days later. This insomnia as a result of my poorly controlled night-time pain is really starting to cause issues. I rarely sleep past half two in the morning anymore and I am not sure how much longer I can sustain my current activity levels on so little sleep. I have some questions for DtM. Has the stent descended further compared with the scan in December? If it hasn't then I don't think we can really blame it for my recent symptoms. What procedure would be involved? Urology versus Interventional Radiology. He obliges with answers a few days later. The stent has not moved any further. Good job I asked, so no need for invasive procedures just yet which is a relief. We throw a few ideas around about therapeutic strategies during an email exchange whilst I am at work.

I have already thought long and hard about the aetiology of the pain. Clinically it feels like a visceral pain. It is not particularly colicky in nature and doesn't have any classical neuropathic pain features. Although it is not really consistent with ureteric spasm I have tried treating it like renal colic with NSAIDs again which were not particularly effective and exacerbated my haematuria. I suppose alpha blockers would also be a possibility if it is ureteric spasm but my blood pressure is not good enough for me to tolerate these. Ever since I was poisoned with ifosfamide I have struggled with postural hypotension and my systolic blood pressure is rarely above 100mmHg these days. I now have to eat more salt and take my time getting up to make sure I am not fainting all over the place. DtM suggests anticholinergics in case the symptoms are bladder spasm related. He forgets I already take solifenacin. He suggests trying something "dirtier", by this he means a less selective anticholinergic agent, but I am reticent about this idea as my urgency and frequency symptoms are well controlled on the solifenacin without any noticeable side effects and I do not particularly want a dry mouth, blurred vision or constipation thank you very much.

I left a message for my Palliative Care Consultant earlier in the week and today she gets back to me. She is a brilliant lateral thinker and has some ideas that had not crossed my mind. She kindly offers to see me the following day, which considering she doesn't usually see outpatients is incredibly generous of her. We have a nice 'catch up' chat about what I have been up to and she has remembered lots of details about my life even though we have only met once before and that was four months ago. She is very keen to try and work out the aetiology of the pain in order to give the best advice regarding treating it. She examines my back in case the pain is referred from there but it doesn't seem to be. My tummy remains very tender on the left and she wonders if she can feel a mass, although this does not correlate with the scan findings which she has reviewed too. It is difficult to come up with a logical answer as to why I am suffering so much at the moment despite all her effort and she admits she is struggling to explain my symptoms. I appreciate her honesty. Sometimes in Medicine there are no answers.

Instead of a lecture about pharmacology we have a sensible discussion about the options and she negotiates with me so effectively. We decide a trial of TENS and Pregabalin would be a good idea instead of just cranking up the opiate doses and turning me into a zombie. I am much more on board with this plan. She tells me that sometimes visceral pain that is not opioid responsive will respond to an adjunctive neuropathic agent as there is usually an element of nerve related pain involved in most visceral pains. A top tip that I will remember the next time I have a patient with difficult to control visceral sounding pain. She gives me her mobile number. It is so reassuring to know I have a direct line to someone so competent, helpful and caring if I need her. I guess she knows I will not abuse this courtesy.

I phone the GP surgery to make an appointment when I arrive home from the hospital to get my prescription. The receptionist tells me she has seen me in the paper, but was disappointed to miss my television appearances. I cannot even make an appointment *in cognito* anymore. The GP visit a few days later is quite amusing. It is a doctor I haven't met before as I would have had to wait ten days to see my usual GP and all I want is a prescription. "I'll keep this short and sweet; please can I have a script for Pregabalin 25mg BD?" "Ok" she responds and prints the paperwork. I am out of the door in under a minute. There is nothing like sticking to the patient's agenda.

Breaking bad news

I have been looking after a lovely gentleman for a number of weeks. He presented to hospital with a gradual onset right sided hemiparesis and a probable focal seizure. He has landed up on the Stroke Unit and perhaps unsurprisingly given his symptoms his CT head has shown a left parietal tumour with surrounding vasogenic oedema. His staging CT has shown a large bronchogenic carcinoma with liver metastases. He is Performance Status four and he has been deteriorating day by day in hospital. On the Unit we have a different Consultant ward round every day to ensure that all the new patients have a Consultant review within twenty four hours of admission. Unfortunately this system, although necessary for reasons of patient safety does result in a lack of continuity of care particularly for the more complex medical patients. Therefore no-one senior has actually taken responsibility for telling this patient his news. They have all been skirting around the point. "Something serious", "growth", "mass" have all been mentioned, but nobody has had the guts to use the word "cancer" or to discuss his prognosis with him. Today I decide enough is enough and that it is about time that this fully compos mentis patient knew what was going on with his health if he wants to know.

His next of kin come in at my request and we have the pre breaking bad news chat. They are already aware that we are looking at a palliative situation. They are reluctant to discuss things with the patient at first not wanting to cause him any unnecessary emotional upset, but as I explain surely he has a right to know as much or as little about what is going on as he wants to and if we do not explore this with him then we are denying him the chance to prepare for his own death. They agree.

We all go together to his side room. I sit next to his bed and take his hand. After a deep breath I ask what he understands so far about his illness and how much he wants to know. Although frail he is completely all there mentally. He wants to know everything. I think he has an inkling what I am about to say. With as much compassion as I can muster after an appropriate warning shot I tell him he has advanced lung cancer that we are not going to be able to treat as he is just too poorly. He is fighting the tears. I gently rub one arm whilst his nephew rubs the other. "It's ok to cry". He lets go and is in floods of tears. I struggle hard not to cry myself. We allow some quiet time for the news to settle. He thanks me for my honesty and I make myself available for later in the day to chat again. He dies three days later, unfortunately in hospital and not at home as he had wished to, but he was comfortable and peaceful and had had the opportunity to update his will and see his family and friends.

It's never easy to break bad news in a compassionate way. It's never easy to receive bad news, I should know. Every time I break bad news now I am reminded of my initial illness presentation. I try and avoid replaying the less than ideal examples of communication I was exposed to and to try to adopt all the good skills I witnessed. The task also makes me reflect on telling Chris and the family about the nightmare as it unfolded and how I used my clinical communication skills to get through doing this. At the time I wanted to be in charge of breaking news to those closest to me and did not want other healthcare professionals to be involved. I'm not entirely sure why this was, perhaps my control freakiness or perhaps an unfounded fear that the communication would be handled badly. I hope that given my experiences I have now become more adept at this crucial task and can perhaps understand the impact of bad news on the individual patient a little better. I seem to have adopted the role of chief 'breaker of bad news' on the ward and I really don't mind. Although it is emotionally draining having time to get it right is a luxury I am fortunate to have in my working day and I find it strangely satisfying.

Realism

Living a cancer story in the public eye as I am now doing, quite by accident and not by design inevitably sparks interest from various different parties. I have been receiving lots of mail from strangers suggesting miracle cures for cancer. Acai berries, force fields, mistletoe, natural healing, tumour eradication chemicals, I've had the lot. Some of the people who have been contacting me are quite persistent and determined to get in touch.

One chap who had metastatic melanoma even phoned one of my bosses and talked to him trying to get my contact details. He went to the National Cancer Institute in the US where they enrolled him in a trial and is alive with clear scans four years later. I am genuinely pleased for him that he has found a solution to his disease but when he sends me all the information about the hoops you have to jump through to even be considered for an NCI trial I just cannot be bothered. The thought of flying to and from the US every few months is not really something I want to even envisage either. I have never shied away from the palliative nature of my condition and have always accepted it. I'm not sure I could deal with all the false hope or raise the hopes of people around me that I would be that miracle patient who gets better. I am too much of a realist. I cannot help feeling that my disease has not progressed in the last few months because I am exercising regularly, staying positive and eating a healthy balanced diet and that I was lucky to have a chemo-sensitive tumour. Miracle cures don't happen to normal folk like me.

Another guy suggests a 'technology' he has developed with a friend that he claims to cure all types of cancer and degenerative diseases without involving surgery or drugs. Apparently it is over 12000 years old and activates stem cells into killing off rogue tumour cells. He seems very upset about my scepticism and desire not to become one of his guinea pigs. I wish him well with his research though. If his claims are true then he will definitely be in line for the Nobel Prize for Medicine and good luck to him, but I just want to get on with living my life.

Professional Courtesy

Chris is away for a few days in Inverness with work and I wake up at 1.30am not with my usual abdominal pain but instead with quite severe right sided pleuritic chest pain. It is very uncomfortable but I don't feel particularly breathless. Me being me I try to ignore it. I don't really want to contemplate the possibility of a PE even though I am fully aware that I am at risk. I have had an upper respiratory tract infection for the past couple of days so I keep telling myself it will just be viral pleurisy or perhaps musculoskeletal chest pain. I struggle through the rest of the night and typical of my usual stoical attitude take myself off to work in the morning. I am in a lot of pain as I walk onto the ward and I must look a bit grey as all the nurses start fussing. They do an ECG which worryingly shows a partial RBBB and my pulse is 120bpm. Oh dear maybe I have had a PE. I am marched up to the ED by one of our stroke researchers as I refuse to get in a wheelchair. This is one of my worst nightmares, getting poorly whilst at work. As I have said before I try to keep the fact I am also a patient separate from my professional life as much as is possible.

We bump into one of the Acute Medicine Consultants who I know well on our way to the ED. I show him my ECG. He is very kind, takes me to the GPAU and finds me a room. Unfortunately he has to dash off to a poorly patient on the CCU but asks one of the other Consultants to see me. My cancer is common knowledge now and it is slightly strange that everyone knows my medical history by having read my book. I give the Consultant a brief run down of the morning's events and a nurse pops by to do another ECG. The Consultant then examines me. Whilst he is auscultating my chest one of the male SHOs who I know comes by to do my cannula and bloods. The Consultant says "it's alright, come in". No it is most certainly not alright and please do not come in whilst I've got my boobs out. I struggle to cover myself up. The SHO quickly scarpers. I don't think it even crossed the Consultant's mind how embarrassing this is for me just letting him examine me without having to go through the indignity of more people than necessary, especially male junior doctors, seeing me undressed.

They arrange for a chest X-ray and CTPA. I only just had a CT a couple of weeks ago and at this rate I am going to glow in the dark! The SHO is great and inserts a green cannula on his first attempt. I'm sure he must be nervous, I would be. He makes a little blood bath taking my blood samples, but I don't care as I am so impressed he has secured decent intravenous access without multiple stabbings. After my X-ray which looks lovely and normal I sit in the GPAU waiting room. Several Consultants pop by to see how I am. I have a little snooze as I am so knackered and I am drowsy having drugged myself up with a little Oxynorm. The other patients in the waiting room are not being particularly patient. They are all winding each other up about having to wait ages for investigations and their perceptions that the hospital is not well organised. They also seem desperate to share their own ideas about what is wrong with them and each other. This is not a discussion I wish to become part of so I am very pleased when my boss turns up and suggests I hide out on the Stroke Unit until they are ready for me in the CT department. My friend's husband who is a Radiologist at the hospital is trying to expedite things for me, but it is a very busy day.

This is my sixth CT scan. I am well used to the routine. No I'm not pregnant. Yes I can confirm my date of birth and address. The CT radiographer is lovely and very experienced. I have seen her name many times on CT head reports but have never actually met her before. I am positioned and scanned initially. Then the contrast is injected. The flushing warm feeling is much more intense today than I have previously experienced and I feel quite dizzy as the scan is completed. I take my time getting up; a collapsing do would not be good. I'm really not in the mood for anymore fussing.

Straight after the scan I go back to the GPAU to look at the images. I find one of the Acute Medicine Consultants who I probably have most respect for clinically in the hospital. He scrolls through the images and I am pleased to not see any filling defects. He cannot see any either. Excellent, crisis averted. Maybe I was just being a hypochondriac. The thought of having to give myself Clexane injections everyday was not pleasant, but I don't have to now so that's great. It is hard in the context of my illness not to interpret symptoms differently now though. Before I knew I had cancer I would definitely not have sought any medical attention for a similar episode of chest pain, but knowing that I have an active pelvic malignancy completely changed my thought processes.

For the most part I was shown so much professional courtesy today. I felt really quite special despite it being an extremely uncomfortable situation for me to be in. The following day my boss tells me after he saw me he had put batteries in his crash bleep just in case so that he could phone Chris if something bad happened. Crikey I must have looked ill! I remind him there would have been no crash call though in view of my DNACPR order.

To and Fro

I seem to have been coming and going from St James's Hospital an awful lot recently. I also seem to have been having far too much to do with the medical profession in my capacity as a patient over the past few weeks. I'm not particularly impressed with myself for having so many problems and it is about time I sorted myself out. I am feeling a little better thanks to the Palliative Care input and not at the expense of losing my mental clarity, which is so important to me.

Today I meet up with another sarcoma patient who is about my age for coffee before my appointment and after hers. She read my book and saw some of the press stuff which prompted her to email and say how inspiring she felt I was. Even though loads of people keep telling me they think I am inspirational I really cannot see it myself. I am just little old me. We worked out that we shared the same next clinic date and arranged to meet up. She works in the health sector too. Over a cup of coffee we share our experiences of living through chemotherapy, of living with a terminal diagnosis, of the team that look after us and the issues about getting back to work. We have both noticed the same quirks about the sarcoma team members and we also share the same dark humour about cancer. It feels like I have known her for years and if our in-patient chemo had coincided I'm sure I would have been happier in hospital, but I guess at least we have met now and I hope I can stay in touch with my new found cancer buddy.

Clinic is running very late today. I sit in a corner, play with my phone and try to finish some work off for a conference I am presenting at in a fortnight. My public speaking appearances are becoming a frequent occurrence. I am aware of so many folk whispering about me, but I try my best to remain inconspicuous. I guess this is the price of celebrity, albeit Z list. Eventually after a very long hour and fifteen minutes DtM collects me from the waiting room. Unusually he looks a touch on the stressed and harassed side today. I ask if he is ok. He admits to feeling "stretched". I suppose this is true of most people working in the NHS at the moment.

It is nice to report feeling a bit better instead of whinging. I disclose about the little PE scare last week though. My pleurisy is settling nicely and it hardly hurts at all anymore. I still think I might have had a teeny PE that just didn't show up on scan. I haven't had any noticeable adverse effects with the Pregabalin and I am titrating up the dose today. My tummy is less tender than it has been on examination too. I read the full CT report from a few weeks ago for myself as I have not had the opportunity yet. There is nothing I didn't already know, but I like to see these things in black and white for myself. Control freak, but it is my body.

Watchful waiting seems like the most sensible plan of action and that is what he proposes. See him again in six weeks. I have so much on my plate in those six weeks what with several Bucket List trips, Adam and Beth's wedding, more media commitments and social outings that I think the time will fly by.

A bad death

I shouldn't be judgemental but I do have very strong personal views about what constitutes a good death. These revolve around as little medicalisation as possible once the terminal phase of life is recognised by minimising unnecessary invasive investigations and procedures, concentrating on really good symptom control and achieving the patient's preference for their place of care if at all possible. These are the things I would want for myself when the time comes.

We are looking after a man at the moment that has been in and out of hospital for a number of years and I remember seeing him on several occasions in the past. He has multiple co-morbidities, is extremely frail and unfortunately has presented to us with a big stroke. He has not picked up since he was admitted from a conscious level point of view. I sit down with his family and have a 'grim reaper' talk. This is not an easy conversation as they are all convinced that he is going to make a full recovery, although clinically everything is pointing towards the opposite outcome. They are also extremely uncertain about the DNACPR decision that had quite correctly been made by my SHO. I cannot seem to make them accept what is actually happening despite my best efforts but I leave the appropriate DNACPR decision in place. I feel a grave sense of failure following the conversation.

I am off work for the next few days but when I return I see that his name is no longer on the patient list. I enquire what happened. The nurses tell me that one of the Consultants had had a further discussion with the family and revoked the DNACPR decision at the family's request. Unfortunately two days later the patient had crashed and died after a forty five minute resuscitation attempt. I cannot help but think to myself what a brutal horrible way to die, definitely not what I would want for myself or for any of my loved ones. I am really quite upset by the events that were entirely preventable. I guess the converse argument would be that perhaps the family needed to see that everything possible was being done in order to accept the death and be able to grieve naturally. I however feel that the patient must always be our first priority and he must have suffered to some extent during this prolonged futile resuscitation attempt. Whether we as doctors choose to resuscitate someone or not is a medical decision. We do not offer all treatments to all patients and in my mind it is absolutely no different with resuscitation.

A new challenge

It is six months since I came back to work. Being accustomed to usually rotating jobs after this length of time I have started to develop itchy feet and think it is about time that I did something different at work. My self confidence is back to normal now and in the context of my disease being stable I feel up for the challenge. I have very much enjoyed my time on the Stroke Unit, but my working day has become a little monotonous and I am in need of a change, after all who knows how long I am going to be knocking around for.

I am extremely lucky to be able to call all the shots when it comes to what I get up to at work at the moment and decide I would like to work for one of the general Elderly Medicine wards. Fortunately one of the Consultants who I get on very well with and who has been really quite influential in my career does not have a Registrar at the moment. He seems pleased I want to work for him again and I hope I can make his life a little easier by taking some of the strain in terms of communication with relatives, dictation, seeing referrals and supporting his junior doctors.

It is emotional leaving the Stroke Unit. They have all been so fantastic supporting my smooth transition back to work after illness and I have always felt that everyone cared so much about me. They are a little shocked about my desire to move on, which must seem to come a little out of the blue. They don't want me to go but I promise to visit regularly and bring cake when I do. I am excited by the new challenge of a new job and I am sure it will do me good mentally. Everyone seems to enjoy my signature chocolate fudge cake I bake as is tradition when I move wards.

The following day I set foot on my new ward at 7.40am, my usual self-inflicted starting time. I am pleased to see some familiar faces and it is rather like a Pontefract Infirmary reunion, reminding me of how happy I was when I worked there as a brand new Registrar. I spend an hour and a half summarising my new patient's notes. The turnover of patients is significantly slower compared to the Stroke Unit and there are several people with metastatic untreatable cancer. The variety of medical problems is refreshing and my first ward round really challenges my clinical skills and knowledge exactly as I hoped it would. My day is made by a lovely 85 year old lady sat at her bedside on her laptop doing some Internet shopping.

A few days later I am doing a ward round with my new boss. Me being me I am questioning the decision to do an OGD on a very frail lady with dementia who has had some coffee ground vomiting which has now settled. Is this invasive test really necessary? Perhaps not and on reflection he agrees with me. We have a conversation about whether my conservatism and pragmatism as a clinician is more pronounced now I'm ill myself. He thinks it is, but that this is not a bad thing as my reasoning is logical and I can confidently justify my decisions. There are often no right answers in Elderly Medicine.

I continue to love everything about my job and feel energised by the change of scenery. Being a doctor is such a privileged position and having the ability to try and help people when they are at the most vulnerable in their lives is very special. We all have a tendency in the profession to moan about how down trodden we feel and how rubbish the system is, but I now try to remember everyday how lucky I am to have such a wonderful career.

Life goes on

The 29th July 2012, exactly one year since I was initially admitted to hospital in California and discovered I had cancer, I wake up next to Chris in a hotel bed on the morning after Adam and Beth's wedding. Predictably given the partying that occurred last night I am hung-over and my feet hurt.

A year ago who'd have thought what would have happened to us over the past twelve months? Life has changed beyond all recognition. I have come pretty close to dying on occasion, I managed to survive some pretty hard-core, unpleasant cancer treatment seemingly suffering every complication under the sun, despite all the odds I have returned to work, I am now an author and Z list celebrity raising a substantial amount of money for the Yorkshire Cancer Centre along the way and we have had some of the most wonderful and exhilarating experiences of our lives as part of the Bucket List.

I have been blessed with disease stability for a much longer time period than any of us would have expected and I am incredibly thankful for so many aspects of my life including my wonderful family, friends and colleagues, and a profession I love that gives me a sense of purpose. I will continue to add to and chip away at my Bucket List concentrating on always living my life to its fullest. I am determined to keep smiling and remembering that there are many people out there far worse off than me.

Life is far too short.
To be sad.
To be mad.
To hold regret.
To look back.
To be depressed.
To be unkind.
Be nice and do good.
Everyday is new.

Who knows how long I have left but I will continue, as a famous song says to always look on *The Bright Side* of life...

Glossary

Adnexa	Where the ovaries and Fallopian tubes are located in a lady
Aetiology	The cause of an illness
Alpha blocker	Drugs that block the alpha receptors in the body and can be used to treat high blood pressure or to relax smooth muscles such as in the urinary tract
Analgesia	Pain relief
Ante-cubital fossa	Where the skin creases at the elbow, the most common place used for taking blood samples
Antegrade ureteric stent	A tube inserted into the ureter from the kidney to relieve a blockage
Anterior	Medical term for in front
Anterior Superior Iliac Spine	Where the hip bones stick out at the front of the body
Anticholinergic	A medication that blocks acetylcholine, which is a type of neurotransmitter, most commonly used to treat overactive bladder
Anticoagulation	Thinning the blood
Anti-emetic	Medication to relieve nausea and vomiting
Arthralgia	Pain and stiffness in joints
Aspiration Pneumonia	An infection in the lungs caused by secretions and/or food/fluids being aspirated in to the lungs when swallowing is impaired
BD	Medical speak for twice a day
Benzodiazepines	Medications used to relieve anxiety and for sedation
Bronchogenic Carcinoma	Doctor speak for lung cancer
Cannulation	Insertion of a small plastic tube into a vein so that medication and fluids can be given intravenously
CCT	'Certificate of Completion of Training', a certificate awarded once training is completed and a doctor can become a Consultant
Cerebellum	The back part of the brain, mainly concerned with balance and co-ordination
Cheyne-Stoking	A pattern of respiration alternating between slow and fast, which is most commonly seen very near to the end of life
Cisplatin	A type of chemotherapy drug
Clexane	A type of heparin which is used to thin the blood and treat blood clots
Clinical Oncology	The cancer specialty concerned with the delivery of radiotherapy
Codeine	A type of weak opiate, primarily used to treat pain

Coronal views	An anatomical description where a vertical plane is used to divide the body
Cortical thickness	When referring to the kidney indicates the amount of functional tissue
Creatinine	A blood test used to look at kidney function (usual range 60-100)
CSF	Cerebro-spinal fluid – the fluid within the ventricles of the brain and surrounds the spinal cord
CTPA	A CT scan specifically looking for a blood clot on the lung
Dacarbazine	A type of chemotherapy drug
Diamorphine	A strong injectable opiate used mainly in Palliative Care
Diuretic	A medication used to off load excess fluid from the body
DMARDs	Disease-modifying anti-rheumatic drugs – medications used in conditions affecting the joints such as rheumatoid arthritis to slow disease progression
DNACPR	Do not attempt Cardio-Pulmonary Resuscitation, a decision made not to attempt to restart the heart if someone suffers a cardiac arrest by using chest compressions, electric shocks and other means
ECG	Electrocardiogram – a tracing of the electrical activity of the heart
ED	Emergency Department – the newer term for A&E
Emetogenic	Causes nausea and vomiting
Fentanyl	A strong opiate medication used for pain relief – usually given by a patch or injection
FSH/LH	Hormones produced by the pituitary gland in the brain that regulate the reproductive organs, high levels in a woman usually indicate the menopause
FY1	Foundation Year 1 doctor – a doctor in their first year of practice
FY2	Foundation Year 2 doctor – a doctor in their second year of practice
GCS	Glasgow Coma Scale - a scoring system used to determine a patients conscious level, ranges from 3 (completely unresponsive) to 15 (fully alert and orientated)
GIM	Abbreviation for General Internal Medicine
Glioblastoma Multiforme	A type of malignant brain tumour
GPAU	GP Assessment Unit – where patients with medical problems referred to hospital by their GPs are assessed

GTN	A type of medication used to treat angina and heart failure
Hemiparesis	Weakness affecting one side of the body – typically after a stroke
Hickman line	An intravenous line inserted into a neck vein and tunnelled under the skin, most commonly used to administer chemotherapy
HPA	Health Protection Agency – mainly involved in Public Health such as controlling the spread of infectious diseases such as meningitis
Hydrocephalus	Accumulation of too much fluid within the brain causing a rise in pressure inside the skull
ICU	Intensive Care Unit
Ifosfamide	A type of chemotherapy drug
Ileostomy	A type of stoma where the small intestine is brought to the surface of the abdomen in an operation, usually performed to relieve an obstruction further along the gut
IMCA	Independent Mental Capacity Advocate – a person who speaks on behalf of a patient who lacks capacity who has no family to ensure the healthcare team are acting in the patient's best interests
INR	International Normalised Ratio – a measure of how thin someone's blood is, used to monitor treatment with warfarin
Intensivist	An anaesthetist who specialises in looking after patients on the Intensive Care Unit
Interventional Radiology	The specialty within Radiology that is concerned with doing procedures using imaging such as X-rays, Ultrasound or CT scans
Intracerebral haemorrhage	Bleeding within the brain
Intubation (tracheal)	Insertion of a tube into the windpipe to artificially help a patient to breathe.
Irinotecan	A type of chemotherapy drug
Laparotomy	A big abdominal operation
LCP	Liverpool Care Pathway, a care pathway used in the final days of life to promote standardised good quality Palliative Care
Levomepromazine	A type of anti-sickness medication
LTFT	Less than Full Time trainee – a doctor completing their training part-time
Lumbar puncture	A procedure where a needle is inserted into the back to obtain fluid from around the spinal cord, used to diagnose meningitis, bleeding in the brain and other neurological conditions

Lymphadenopathy	Describes enlarged lymph nodes, most commonly seen in cancer and infections
MAU	Medical Admissions Unit
Medical Oncology	The cancer specialty concerned with giving chemotherapy
Metastases	When cancer has spread from its original site to a distant organ such as the liver or the brain
Metronidazole	An antibiotic
MEWS	Modified Early Warning Score – a scoring system combining a patient's observations such as their pulse and blood pressure, which should alert nurses and doctors to a clinical deterioration
Midazolam	A type of benzodiazepine medication that is used to sedate patients
MRI	Magnetic Resonance Imaging – a type of specialised scan that uses very strong magnets to obtain images of the body
MRSA	Methicillin Resistant Staphylococcus Aureus, one of the common healthcare associated bugs
MSU	Mid-stream specimen of urine, a clean catch urine sample
Mucositis	Inflammation of the mucous membranes such as in the mouth, a common side effect of chemotherapy
Nasal bridle	A device used to keep a nasogastric tube in place
Nasogastric tube	A tube that is inserted through the nose down into the stomach and in stroke care is primarily used to feed patients who are unable to swallow
NBM	Nil by mouth
Nephrostomy	A tube inserted directly into the skin through the skin to relieve an obstruction in the ureter
Neuropathic pain	Pain caused by nerve dysfunction
Neutropaenia	A low neutrophil count
Neutrophil	The most common type of white cell in the blood, important in fighting infections
Non-pharmacological	Without using medications
Nozinan	A type of anti-sickness medication
NSAIDs	Non-steroidal anti-inflammatory drugs, for example ibuprofen, used to treat pain and inflammation
Obstructive uropathy	Kidney failure as a result of a blockage in the urinary tract causing back pressure
OCD	Obsessive Compulsive Disorder
Octaplex	A medication used to reverse the effects of warfarin when a patient is bleeding
OGD	A camera test of the gullet and stomach
OH	Occupational Health

Opiate	A type of pain relieving drug
Oxycontin	A strong long acting opiate medication used to treat pain
Oxynorm	A strong short acting opiate medication used to treat pain
P6 protocol	A chemotherapy regimen developed in the United States and used to treat Desmoplastic Small Round Cell Tumour
PACS	The abbreviation given to the electronic X-ray viewers used in hospitals
PACES	A clinical exam to become a member of the Royal College of Physicians
Pathophysiology	The study of how disease is manifest and how this relates to the normal function of the body
PE	Pulmonary embolism, a blood clot on the lung
PEG	Percutaneous Endoscopic Gastrostomy – a tube inserted into the stomach using a camera so that a patient who cannot swallow safely can be fed long-term
Performance Status	A scoring system to quantify cancer patient's well-being and quality of life, ranges from 0 to 5 (0 is fully active, 4 is bed-bound, 5 is dead)
Peripheral Neuropathy	Damage to the nerves of the peripheral nervous system, most commonly manifest as numbness and tingling in the hands and/or feet
Pharmacology	The study of the action of drugs
Photophobia	Dislike of bright lights, usually seen in patients with meningitis
Pleurisy	Pain caused by inflammation of the pleura, the outer linings of the lungs
PNH	Paroxysmal Nocturnal Haemaglobinuria, a rare blood disorder
Portacath	A small device inserted beneath the skin that allows access to big veins in the neck, can be used in patients who have poor veins in their arms
Posterior	Medical term for behind
Postural hypotension	When your blood pressure goes down when you stand up
Pregabalin	A medication used to treat nerve related pain and epilepsy
PRN	Medical speak for as required
Prophylaxis	Something done to prevent something happening, for example if you are exposed to an infectious disease taking some antibiotics to prevent you becoming infected yourself

Pulmonary oedema	Fluid on the lungs
PV bleeding	Medical speak for vaginal bleeding
Rifampicin	An antibiotic
RBBB	Right bundle branch block, an abnormality seen on a tracing of the heart rhythm (ECG) sometimes indicating a lung problem such as a blood clot
Renal calculi	Kidney stones
Sarcoma	A cancer affecting the connective tissues such as bone, muscle, cartilage, muscle or fat.
Sclerosed	Describes hardened or thickened tissues in the body
SHO	Senior House Officer, a junior doctor
SOCRATES	A mnemonic acronym used to take a pain history (Site, Onset, Charater, Radiation, Associations, Time course, Exacerbating/relieving factors and Severity)
Solifenacin	An anticholinergic medication used to treat overactive bladder
Somatisation	Where psychological distress is manifest as physical symptoms
Subcuticular sutures	Stitches beneath the skin in the subcutaneous tissues, usually result in a better cosmetic outcome
Subdural haematoma	Bleeding into the outer lining of the brain
TACS	Total Anterior Circulation Stroke, a medical term for a severe stroke
Temozolamide	A type of oral chemotherapy drug
TENS	Transcutaneous Electrical Nerve Stimulation - a pain relief method where tiny electrical currents are delivered to the affected part of the body through pads
TPN	Total Parenteral Nutrition, when food is given in a liquid form directly into the veins of patients whose gut is not able to function normally
Tramadol	A weak opiate medication used to treat pain
Ureters	The tubes linking the kidneys to the bladder
Urology	A surgical specialty concerned with the urinary tract
Vasogenic oedema	Swelling seen around brain tumours
Venepuncture	Medical speak for taking blood samples
Vesico-ureteric reflux	When urine tracks back up the ureters from the bladder
Vincristine	A type of chemotherapy drug
Visceral pain	Pain that comes from organs, often described as diffuse, aching, difficult to localise and may be referred to other parts of the body
Vitamin K	A medication used primarily to reverse the effects of warfarin
Warfarin	A medication used to thin the blood

Biography

Dr Kate Granger is a third year Elderly Medicine Registrar working part-time at a busy District General Hospital in West Yorkshire. Kate grew up in Huddersfield where her parents still live but now resides in Wakefield with her husband Chris. She trained at Edinburgh University and graduated in July 2005 with Honours after which she moved back to Yorkshire to get married and begin working. Her main medical interests include education, Palliative Care in the acute hospital setting, continence and the interface between Surgery and Geriatric Medicine. Outside work Kate loves to cook and entertain her friends and family. She enjoys embroidery, playing her flute, cinema, watching cricket and reading. She is also a keen swimmer.

In August 2011 aged just 29 Kate was diagnosed with a very rare and aggressive type of sarcoma. She wrote her first book *The Other Side* during long sleepless nights whilst undergoing treatment for this cancer after being inspired by one of her bosses, Dr Frank Phelan to keep a diary. She has been busily working through her Bucket List since her diagnosis and is pictured here  with Chris at their Renewal of Wedding Vows ceremony, a key event on the list.

A true story of one doctor's journey as a patient coming to terms with a terminal cancer diagnosis. The hope is that healthcare professionals will read it, in particular young doctors and medical students, and understand exactly what being a patient is really like and how their behaviours, no matter how small can impact massively on the people they look after. It is also a story of personal battles with control and learning how and when to relinquish this.

As of August 2012 *The Other Side* has sold nearly 3000 copies raising over £16000 for the Yorkshire Cancer Centre appeal.

What others have said about *The Other Side*:

"Thoughtful, incisive and reading it should be a prerequisite for passing your MBChB."
"I've long felt that every doctor should have personal experience of serious illness. For everyone fortunate enough not to have that experience, there is this book."
"Unputdownable."
"I have no doubt at all that your exceptionally clear, honest and well written book will make me a better doctor."

<u>www.theothersidestory.co.uk</u>

Yorkshire Cancer Centre

 All profits from the sale of both *The Other Side* and *The Bright Side* are being donated to the Yorkshire Cancer Centre, which is the fundraising arm of St James's Institute of Oncology in Leeds, where Kate is being looked after. Each day, the Institute has responsibility for treating 1500 patients from a catchment population of 2.6 million, most of whom will have had a cancer diagnosis. A £10 million appeal was launched in 2007 to fund supplementary benefits such as specialist medical equipment, research and development, patient 'home comforts' and arts and gardens projects.

Bexley Wing atrium, St James's University Hospital, Leeds